Do you acknowledge that you are here by your own ███ ███, that you may leave at any time?

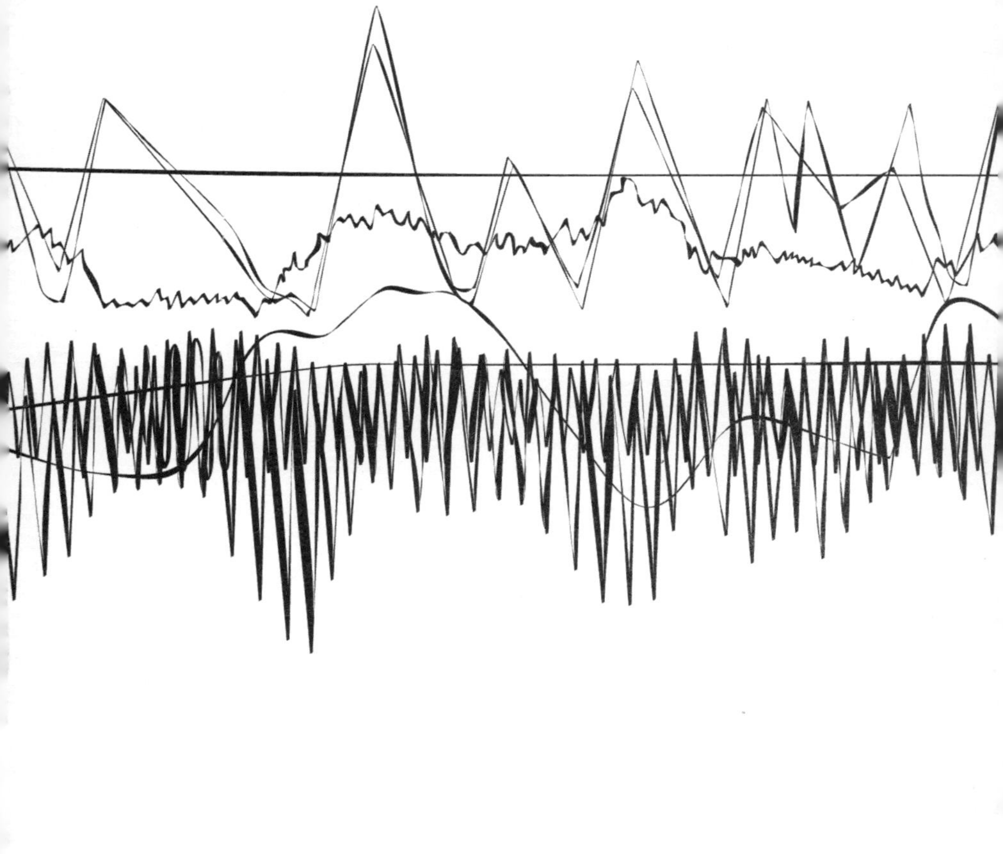

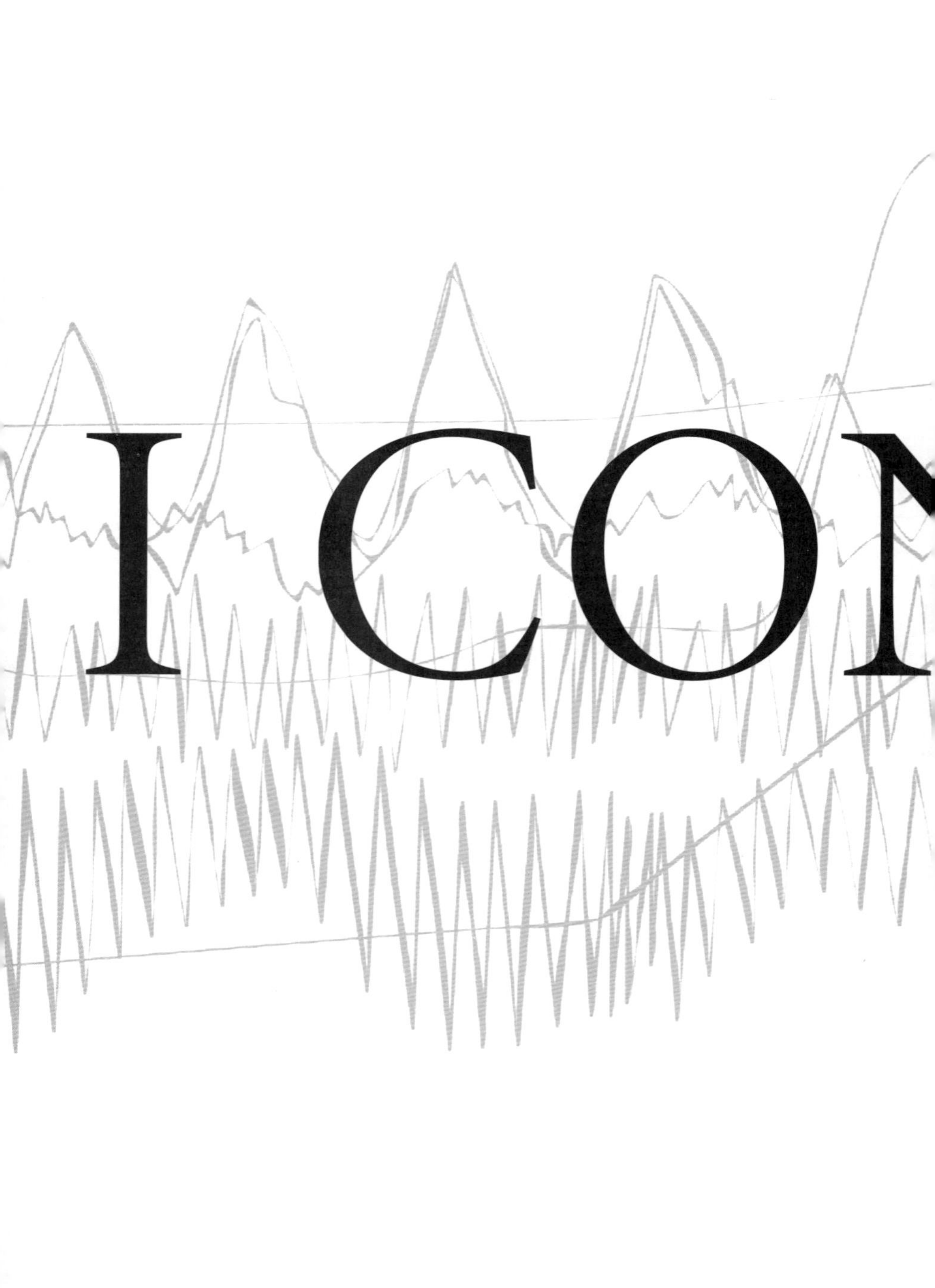
I CON

Eric Schmaltz

Do you solemnly swear that you will tell the ████, the whole ████?
& nothing but the ████ under pains & penalties of perjury?

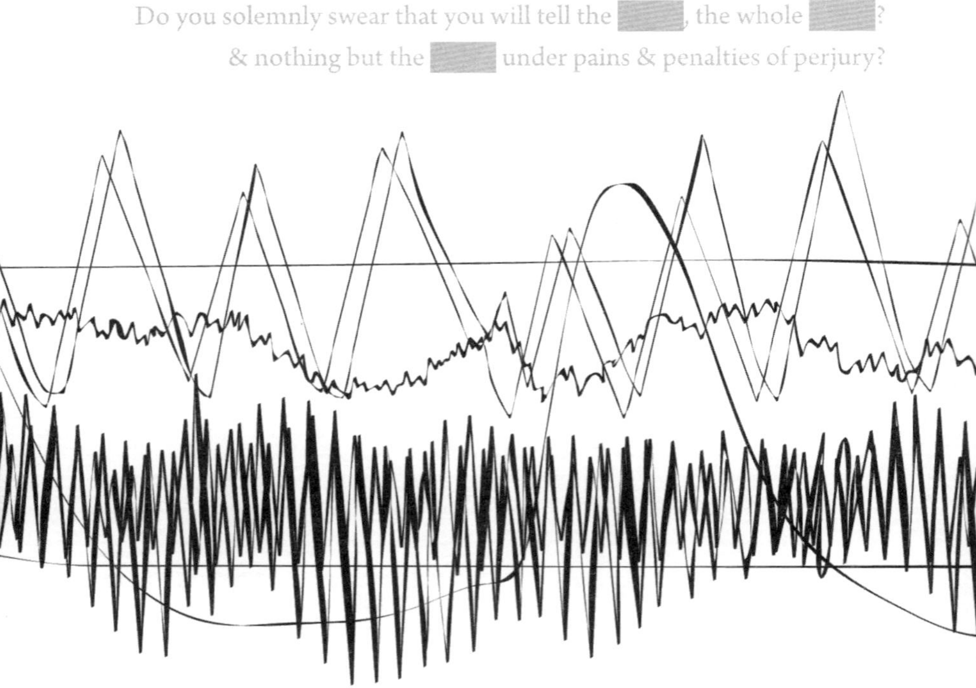

I Confess

Eric Schmaltz

with an afterword
by Orchid Tierney

Place

your

hand

upon

this

book;

repeat

after

me

Coach House Books, Toronto

first edition

Published with the generous assistance of the Canada Council for the Arts and the Ontario Arts Council. Coach House Books also acknowledges the support of the Government of Canada through the Canada Book Fund and the Government of Ontario through the Ontario Book Publishing Tax Credit.

LIBRARY AND ARCHIVES CANADA CATALOGUING IN PUBLICATION

Title: I confess / by Eric Schmaltz with an afterword by Orchid Tierney.
Names: Schmaltz, Eric, author | Tierney, Orchid, author of afterword.
Identifiers: Canadiana (print) 2025023341X | Canadiana (ebook) 20250234599 | ISBN 9781552455111 (softcover) | ISBN 9781770568754 (EPUB) | ISBN 9781770568747 (PDF)
Subjects: LCGFT: Poetry.
Classification: LCC PS8637.C44912 I23 2025 | DDC C811/.6—dc23

I Confess is available as an ebook: ISBN 978 1 77056 875 4 (EPUB), ISBN 978 1 77056 874 7 (PDF)

Purchase of the print version of this book entitles you to a free digital copy. To claim your ebook of this title, please email sales@chbooks.com with proof of purchase. (Coach House Books reserves the right to terminate the free digital download offer at any time.)

A LIAR
A LINE
A LYRE

'The scariest untruths
come from those
who've swayed themselves
from veracity's side
and forget the sway'

– Bart Vautour, *The Truth About Facts*

You do solemnly state that the testimony you may here give shall be the ████, the whole ████, & nothing but the ████?

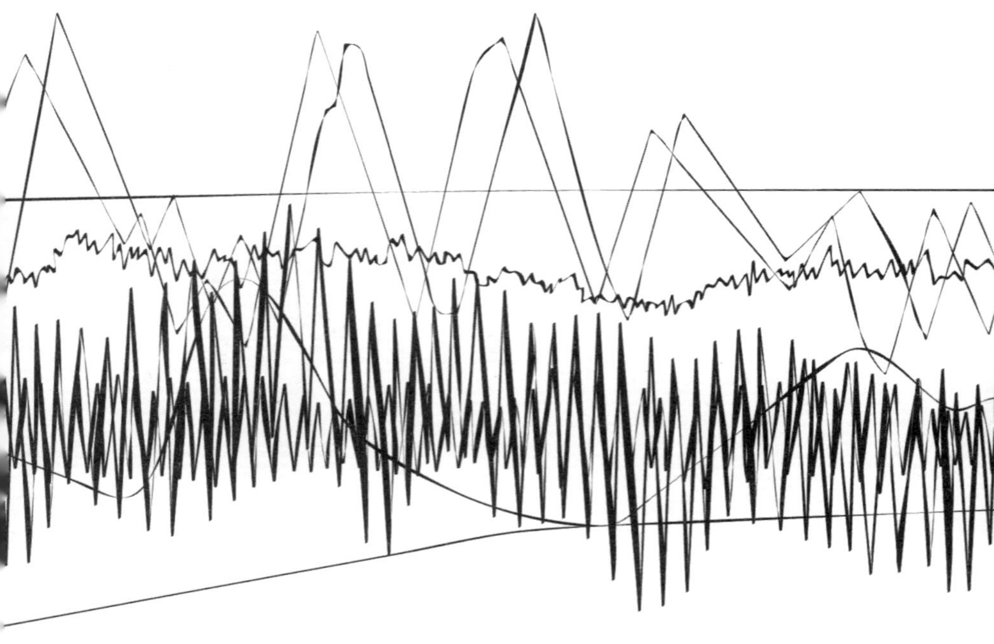

for adp & [redacted]

for judith & paul

So help you ?

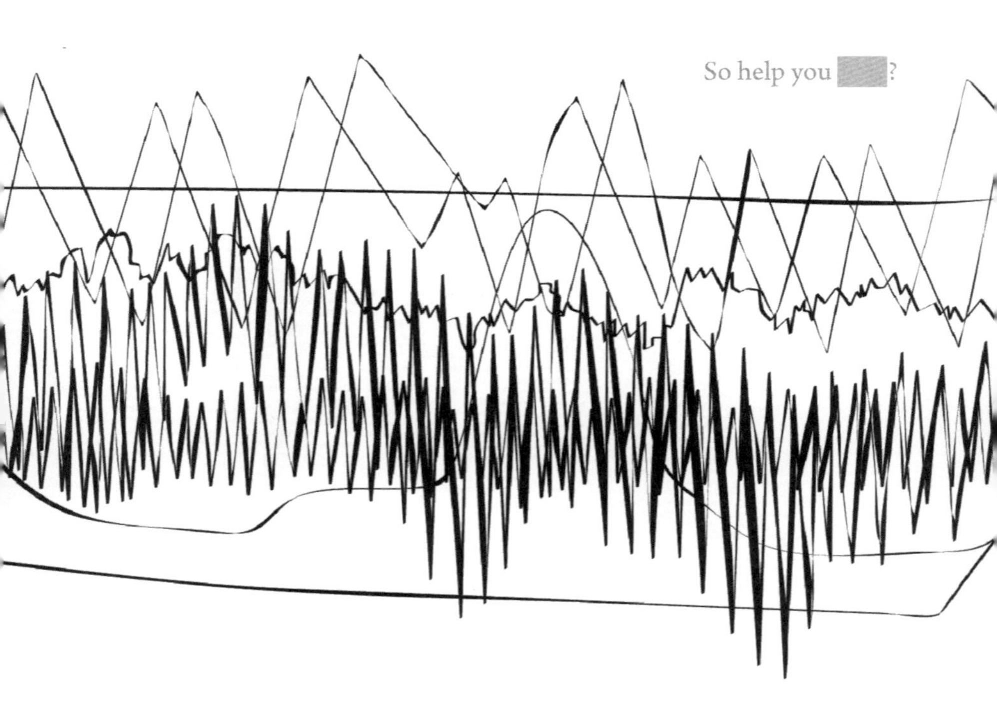

This book is a document of truth's performance under duress.

Some of what you will read is true; the rest is poetry.

Dear Eric,

Thank you for the retainer. The balance owing is $███.██ which you will pay at our polygraph appointment on ██████, ██████ at ██████. As mentioned, the retainer is non-refundable, but you can change the appointment if I receive notice at least ██ ████ in advance. You can only change the appointment one time. Any appointment changes within ██ ████ will be subjected to an additional $███.██ rescheduling fee. If you do not show up to the appointment you will not receive your $███.██ back as it is non-refundable. If you wish to schedule a new appointment outside of ██ ████ after the deposit was received or after a one-time appointment change, then you will be subjected to an additional $███.██ rescheduling fee. Please see the attachment with an outline of the procedure and guidelines for how the test will be conducted. Failure to comply with these items may result in the termination of the examination and full payment of the examination will still be required. My office is located at ██████ ██████, ██████. I have attached office directions. The building looks like ██ ██ ██████, but it has been converted into office space. The front door is the main door for all the offices so please come inside and have a seat in the ██████ ████ when you arrive.

Sincerely,
Emily Cauduro, M.Sc., B.Sc.

Polygraph (n.):

from Greek polygraphos, 'many writings'

Do you acknowledge that you are
here by your own free will and that you
may leave at any point in time?

Yes.

Do you acknowledge that you are here by choice
and that you have not received any threats,
promises of immunity, and that you speak
here today free of any duress, coercion, or force?

Yes.

Do you agree to hold me free from harm,
liability, or legal actions from the results?

Yes.

Good.

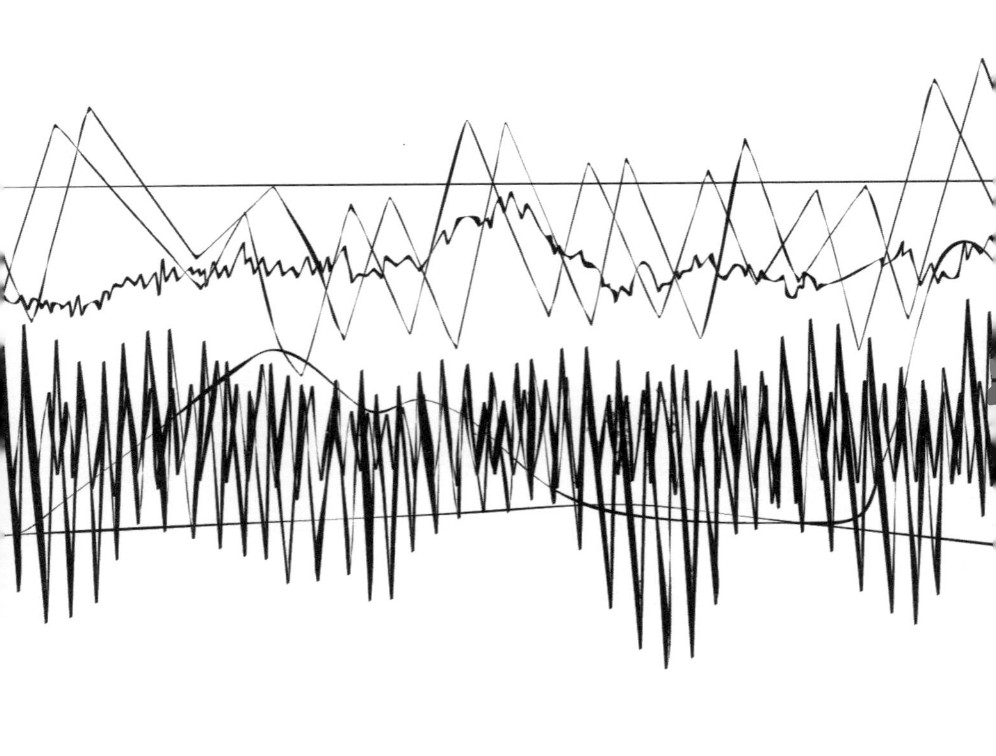

A LIAR
A LINE
A LYRE

'When it is not spontaneous or dictated by some internal imperative, the confession is wrung from a person by violence or threat; it is driven from its hiding place in the soul, or extracted from the body.'

– Michel Foucault, *The History of Sexuality, Vol. 1*

Performative Utterances

Do you acknowledge
that you are here
by your own free will,
that you may leave at any time?
Please place your hand
upon this book; repeat after me

Do you
solemnly swear
that you
will tell the truth,
the whole truth?
& nothing
but the truth
under pains
& penalties
of perjury?

You do solemnly
state that the testimony
you may here give
shall be the truth
the whole truth
& nothing
but the truth
so help you god?

chew on a mouthful of rice
spit it out
chew on bread & cheese
swallow them
lick a hot iron
show me your tongue

walk three paces
over scalding ploughshares
walk three paces
gripping a hot iron
brandish the cross
with one arm
retrieve your ring
from boiling oil
retrieve this stone
from boiling water

swallow & vomit
a peach pit
sink three times
in a water barrel
survive the depths
of the river
cross your pinky
overtop of mine

Trial by Combat

at the threshold, two men train
their blades aloft

two men, back to back, dusk's
resting ombre, guns to their lips

a man & wife, armed,
her weapon sheathed, his drawn

flanked by flags, a man stands, mouth
open, eyes closed, arms askew: save america

a screenshot from game of thrones:
a tendon sliced thru

a fallen man, a shattered
fence, parts strewn

two men, standing,
pole maces clasped

a fallen man, an oak leaf
yellowing, roots & shadow

one man stands holding a severed head,
royalty poised on up above

a screenshot from game of thrones:
blood against the colour of the sky

a fallen man,
another thrusts his spear

flanked by flags, a man stands, mouth
open, eyes closed, arms askew: save america

two men, shields in place,
sharing the sun

a screenshot from game of thrones:
a spear thru a fallen man's heart

flanked by flags, a man stands, mouth
open, eyes closed, arms askew: save america

a fallen man, angels on up
above, flora lies below

Trial by Touch

after *Hamburgisches Stadtrecht von 1497*

a punctum of disorder: all
have left their labour

to gather in the theatre
for the rush of the body's blood.

the accused stands bare
chested & birched as a prelude

to what the dead may sing.
justice is in the surrounds:

those who sin, punish them
in the face of all
so that the rest may fear.

out of sight's line, a man
lifts a woman & the accused lays

down her flayed palms.
all listen for the hymn,

a fluid trickles from
the corpse's lips & so

the accused confesses,
writing it in blood's song

Trial by Fire

after *Peter Igneus Over the Fire*

the hall is soft & angled, a pinkish
pastel before hills of sloping green. he stands

at the centre of the scene in rippling flame,
with its trails tending to his hem,

its pared tongues raising his curtain
for those haloed enough to see. their fingers,

one & two, lines to a god while
his skinny digit crooks inward

or more, toward the room eclipsed
by men, weapons drawn, wanting & having it

in the dark, leaving still, even now, with our
dignities as we watch with distracted eyes.

the will unfurls in the festering of a wound

Trial by Force

Third Degree (n.): The employment of methods which inflict suffering, physical or mental,

upon the subject

upon their shoulders

upon the question

upon these statements

upon the information

upon the testimony

upon the objections

upon his property

upon his neck

upon the face

upon a rock

upon sidewalks

upon our field

upon a printed page

upon the sound

upon the public

upon someone

upon some persons

upon such other persons

upon your own

upon a person who knows

upon a person

in order to obtain information about a crime.

Trial by Voice

Truth peaks while lies plateau. Analyze the following sonographs to determine the the poet's truth-speak.

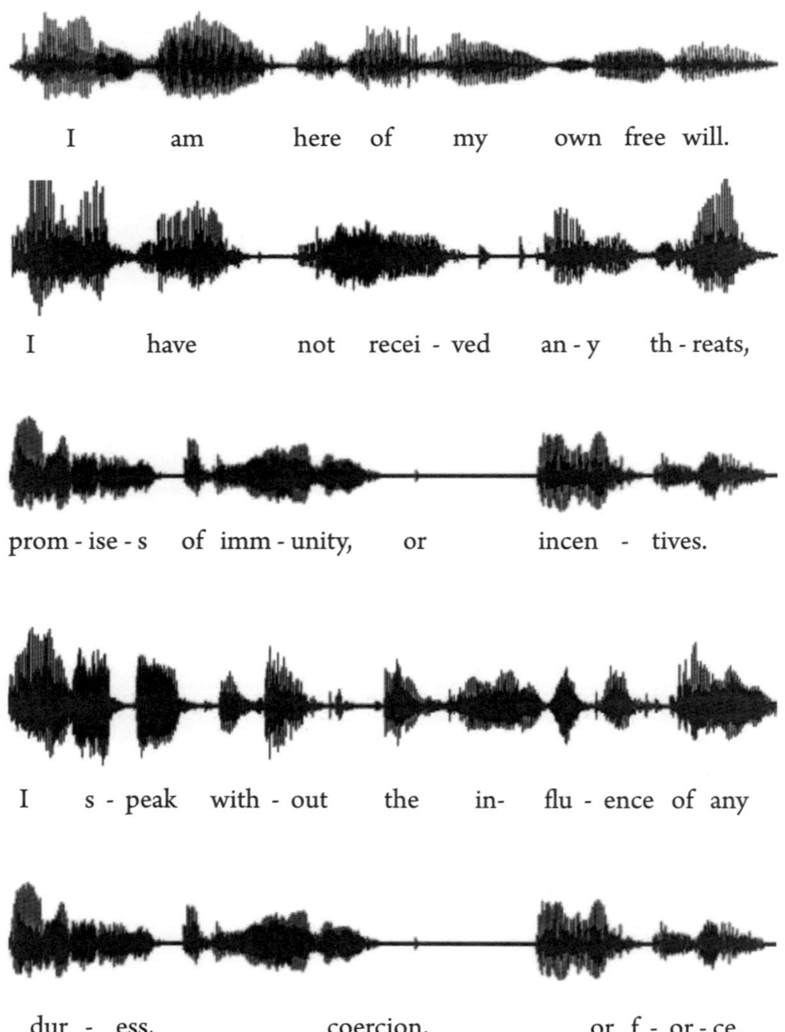

I will f - or - ever hold you free of a - ny harm,

lia - bil - ity cl - aim-s, or leg - al ac - tions flo - wing

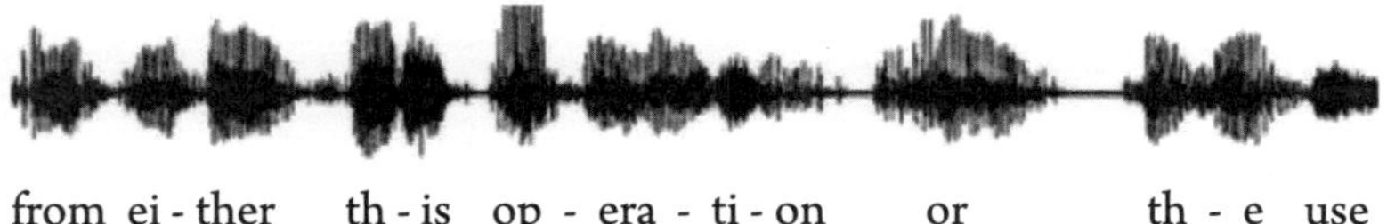

from ei - ther th - is op - era - ti - on or th - e use

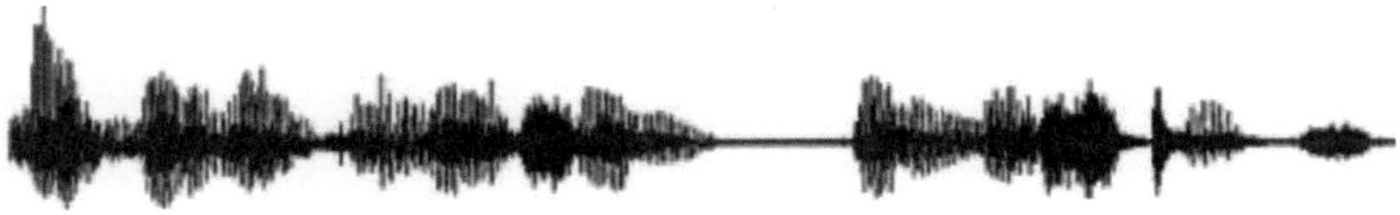

of th - e in - for - ma - tion in th - is t - ex - t.

Trial by Serum

lying beneath the angel's trumpets

my mind would centre upon
the true facts I could not remember

Q. What is your age?
A. – thirty-one.

Q. Where were you born?
A. – in the kitchen on a nail
behind the picture.

beneath the angel's trumpets, I speak
voluntarily without any strength

of will

Trial by Waterboard

the puddles of water
on the floor

where there's an ice
chest filled with water

dips the pitcher
in the chest

hands shaking
starts pouring

pours water
over the towel

so it hits
& water spurts

rain pelts
the brown city, turning
the gutter water black

the water
shimmering
surreal

Trial by Cold Water

'My weight is my love; I am borne by it
wherever I am borne'
– St. Augustine

my lungs brimmed
in my first memory,

chlorinated & sodden I sunk
to the bottom of the pool.

it was no other occasion
than friendship's cusp,

a longing to be accepted
at three, maybe four,

by him, his grandfather,
maybe his mother, the early blue

below, the sky, the clouds,
cirrus, maybe cumulus,

& the concrete's scrape
on my callow knees.

we pulled the cushions, piled
in the living room, maybe the kitchen,

& laid them by the poolside.
I remember the sun but no heat, maybe.

I didn't confess
that I could not

swim. I stepped toward
the pool's limit

it welcomed me in
my purity, weighted

by my longing, by
virtue of my lie

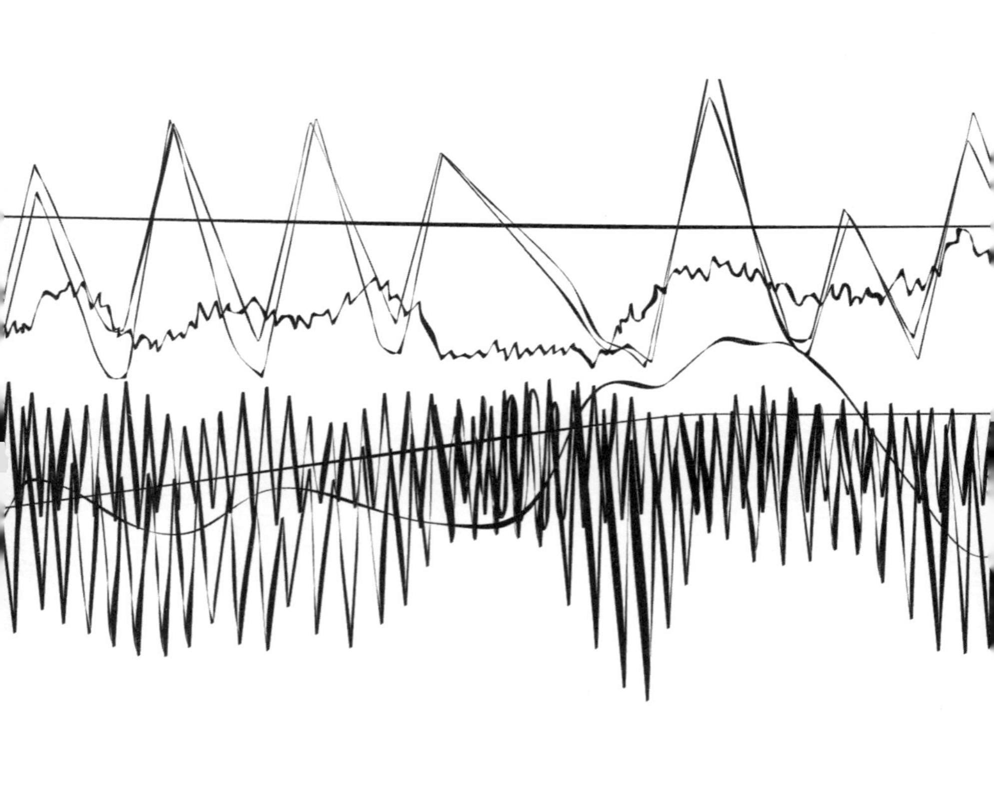

A LIAR
A LINE
A LYRE

‘Tell all the Truth but tell it slant – ’

– Emily Dickinson, ‘1263’

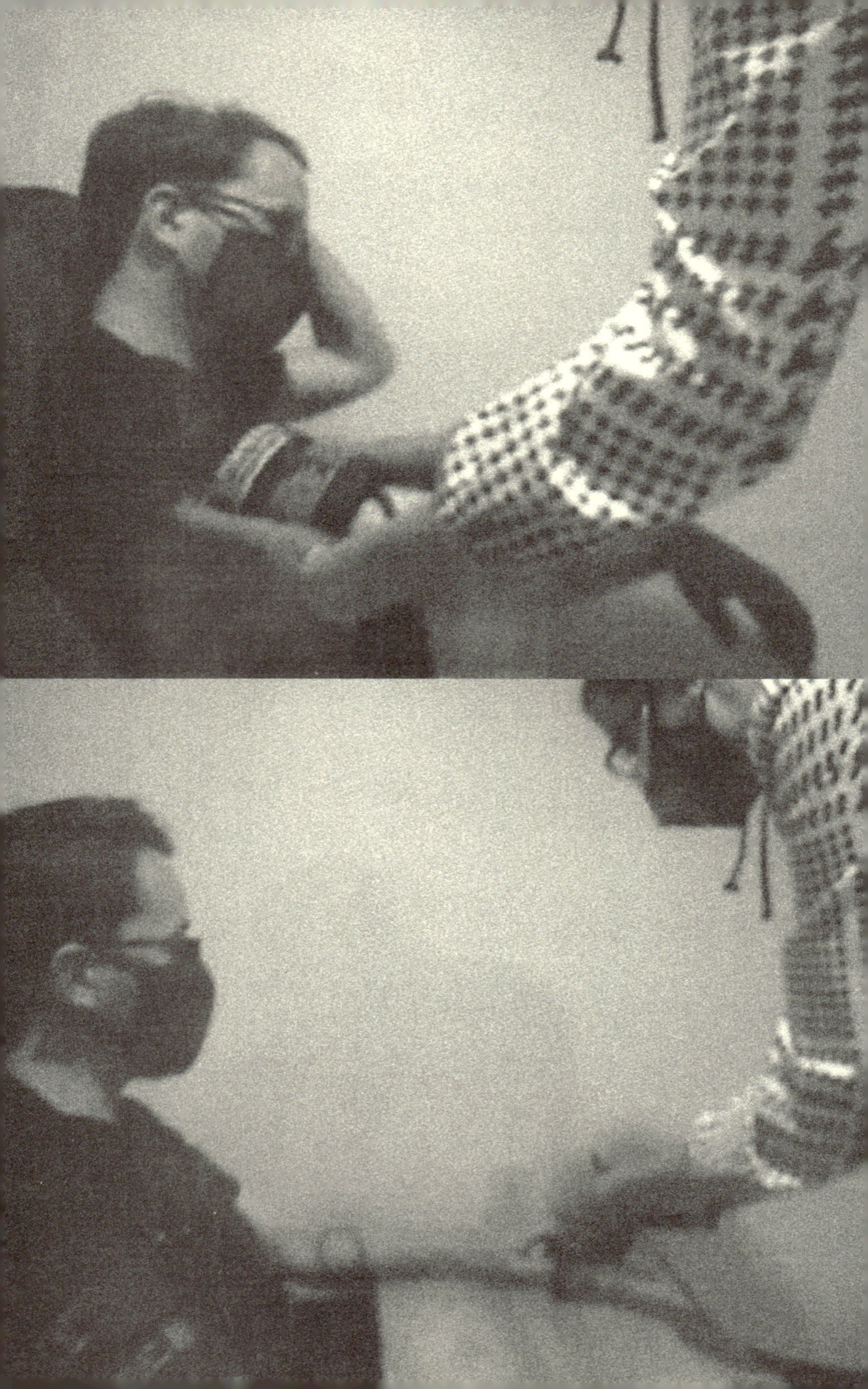

the analyst stands. she slants my back, encircles me with the first hook & eye feel myself ripple. every redaction undoes itself, an intimacy of text & tissue forms at my chest. my breath flutters as she forms my eloquence out of monitors & clasps. the table evaporates into my palms. I meditate on my unwired awareness while the wires promise to lay me bare, to transmute every murmur electric, to descend into the raw & let every bit of me enlighten into lyric. I promise from my skin while the snarl of my truth is veiled.

I'm increasing the blood-pressure cuff. The test is about to begin. Please sit quietly and answer only with yes or no. I will be asking you only the questions we have reviewed or regarding ██████. Do you intend to answer truthfully?

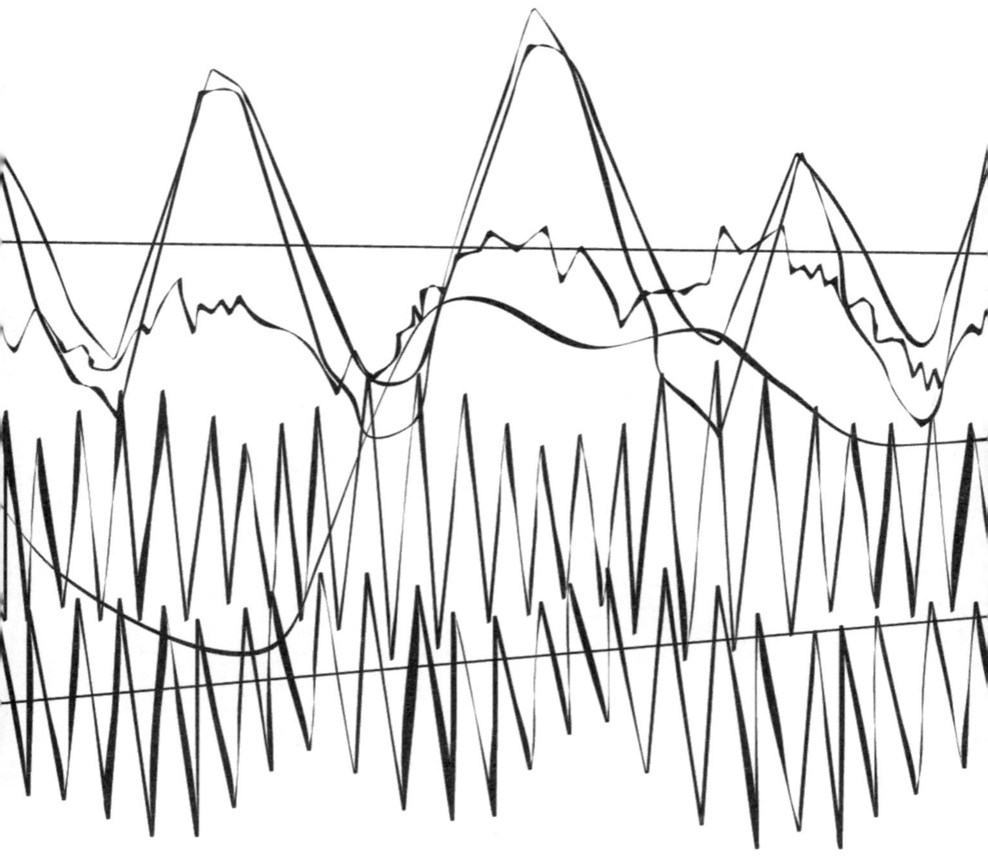

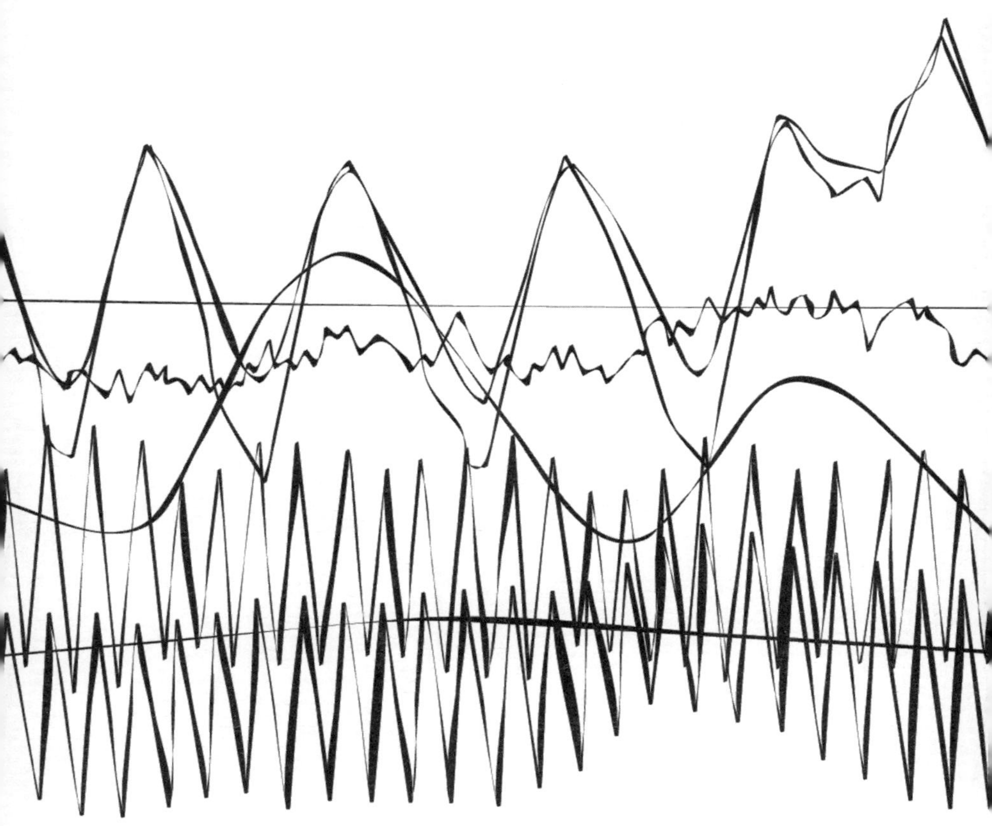

Yes.

Is your name Eric Schmaltz?

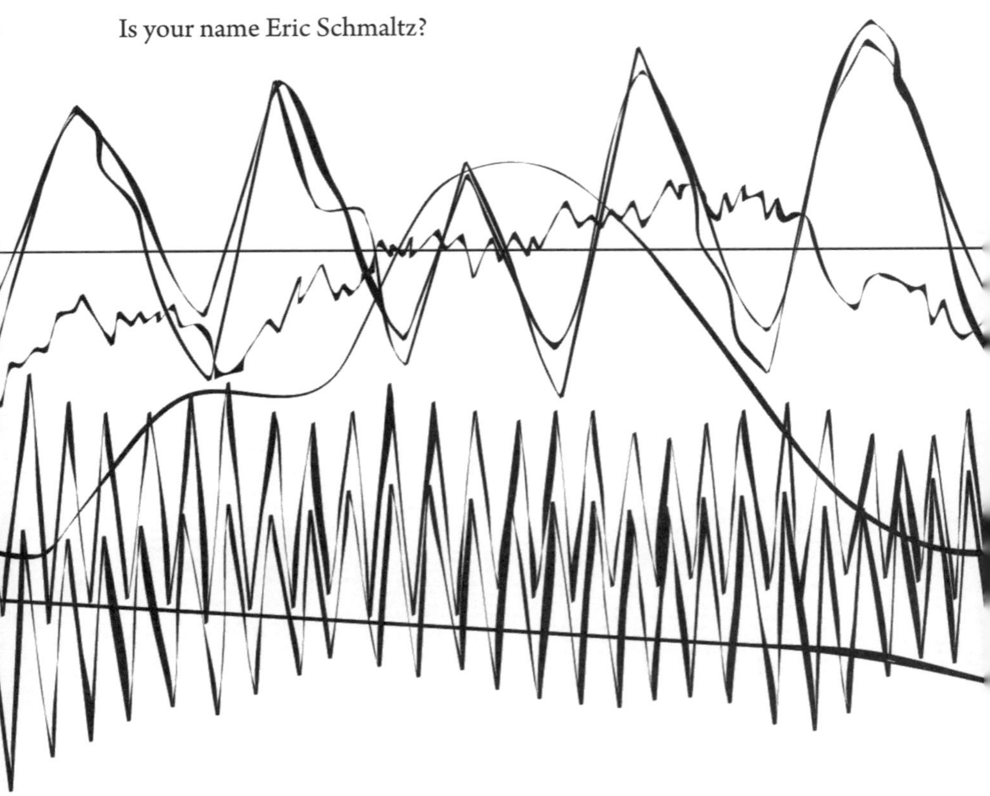

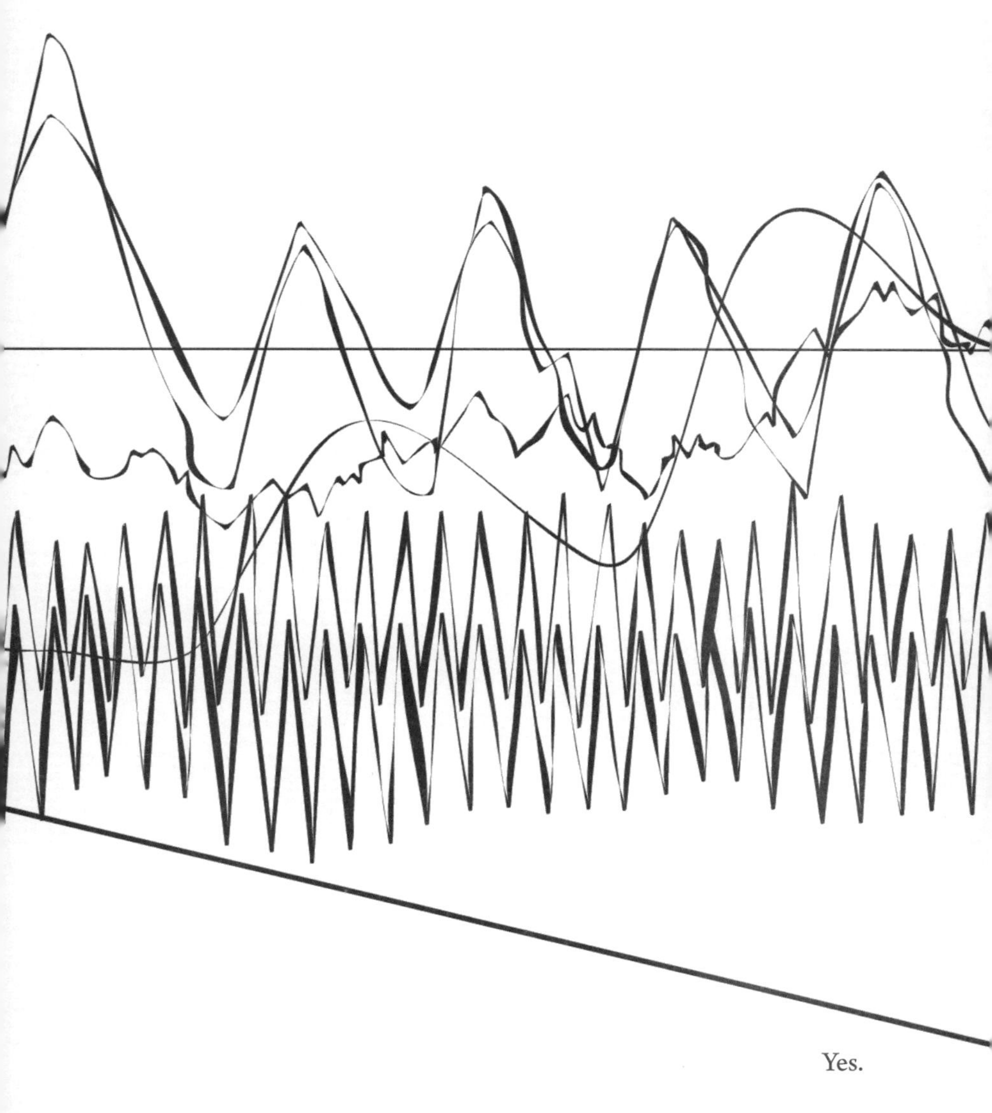

Yes.

Have you ever ████ from █████ without █████ ████?

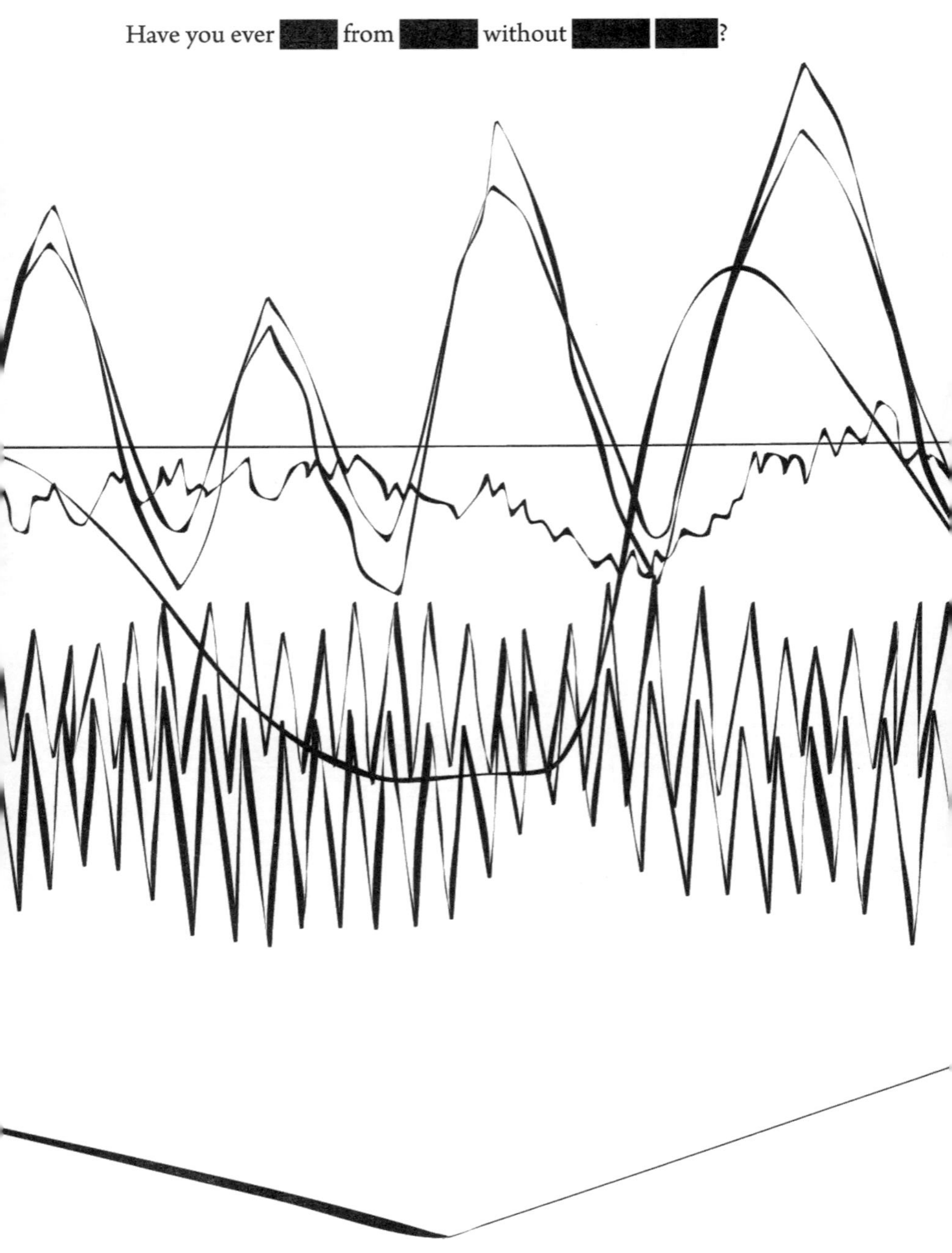

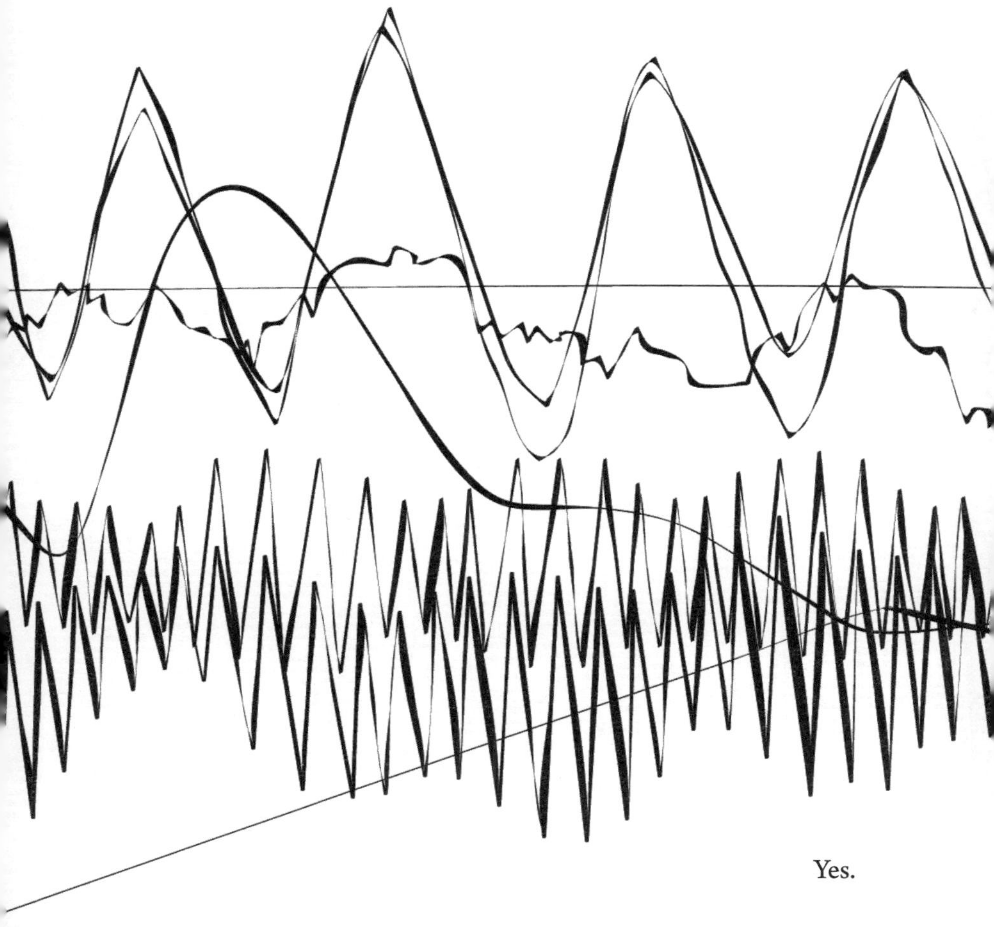

Yes.

Did you intentionally ███ any ███ in the past year?

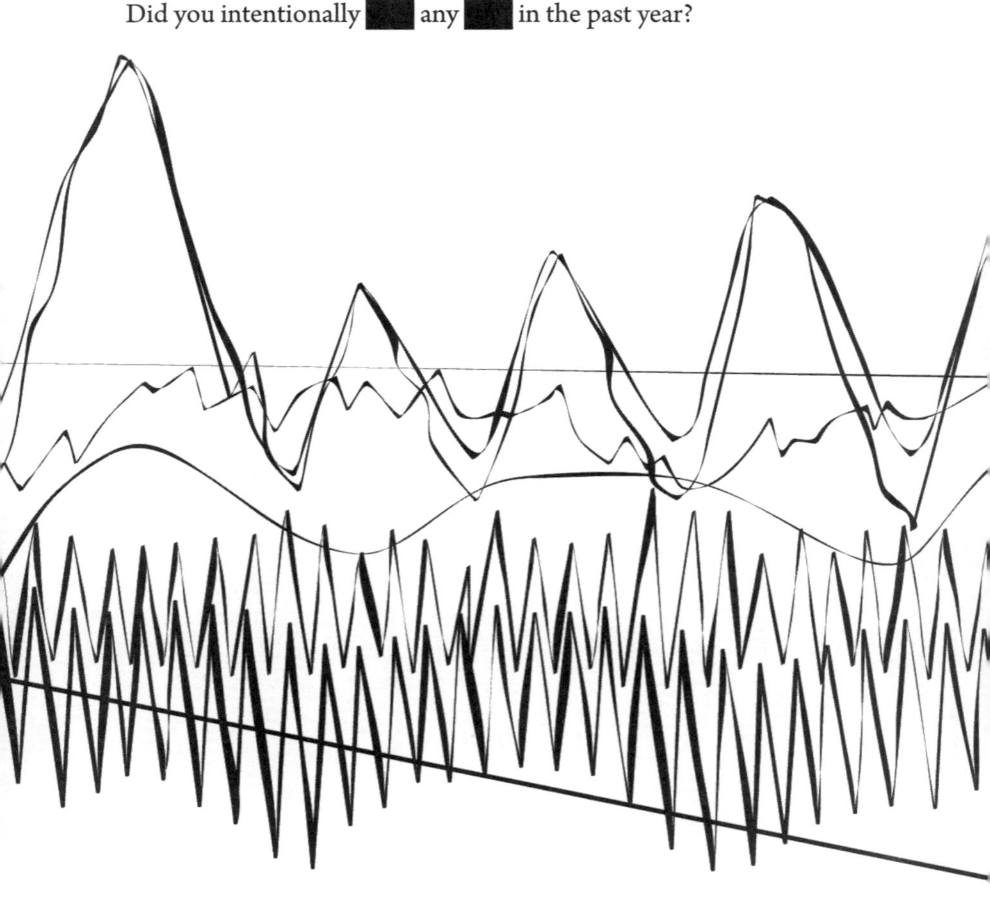

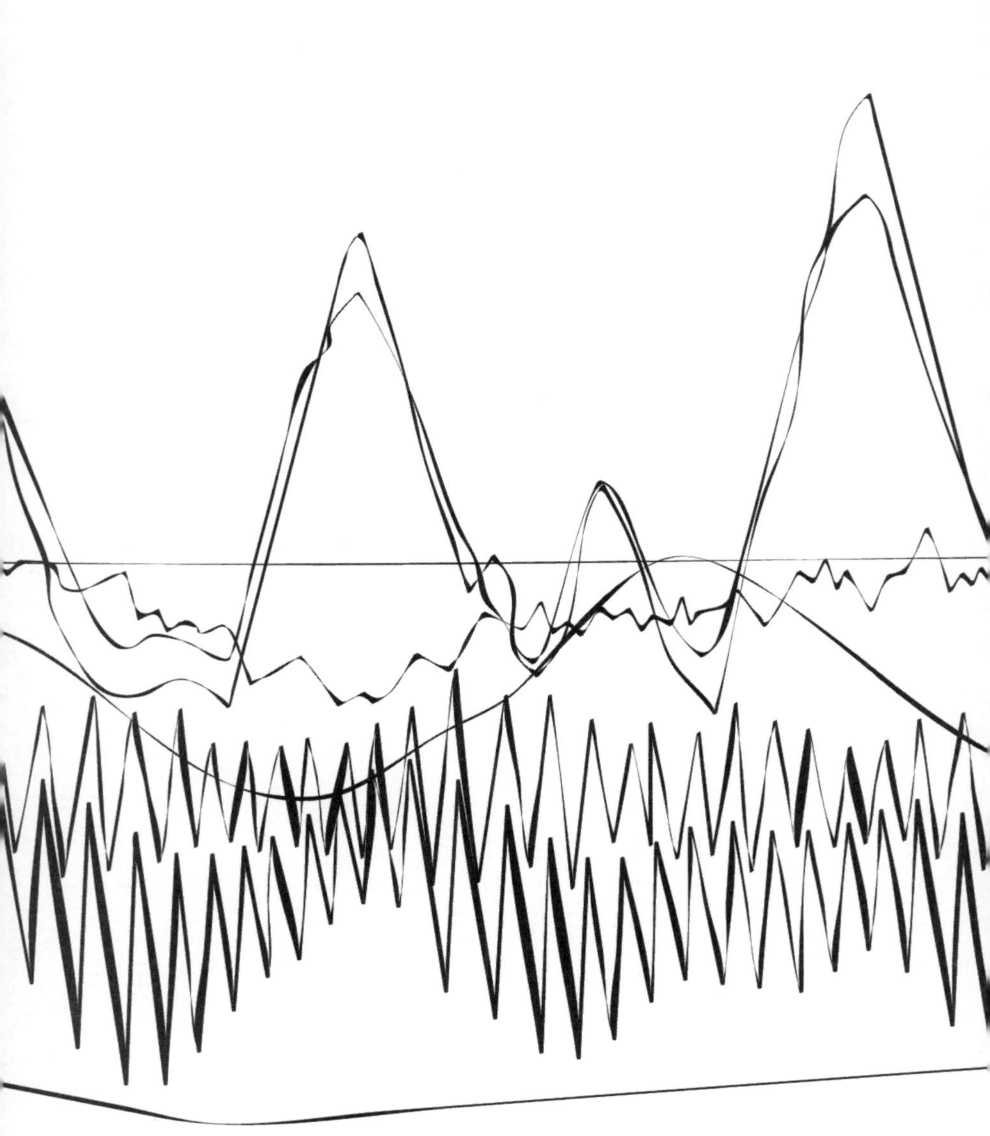

No.

In your whole life, have you ever [redacted] a loved one?

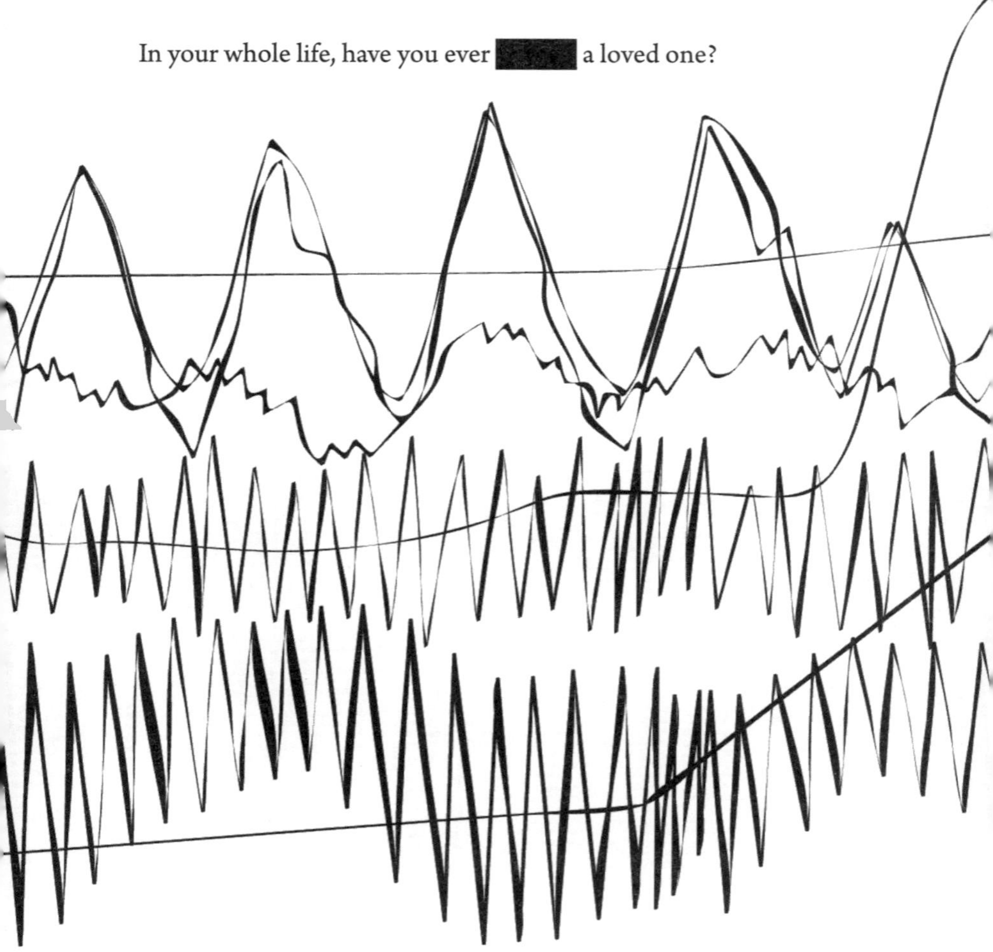

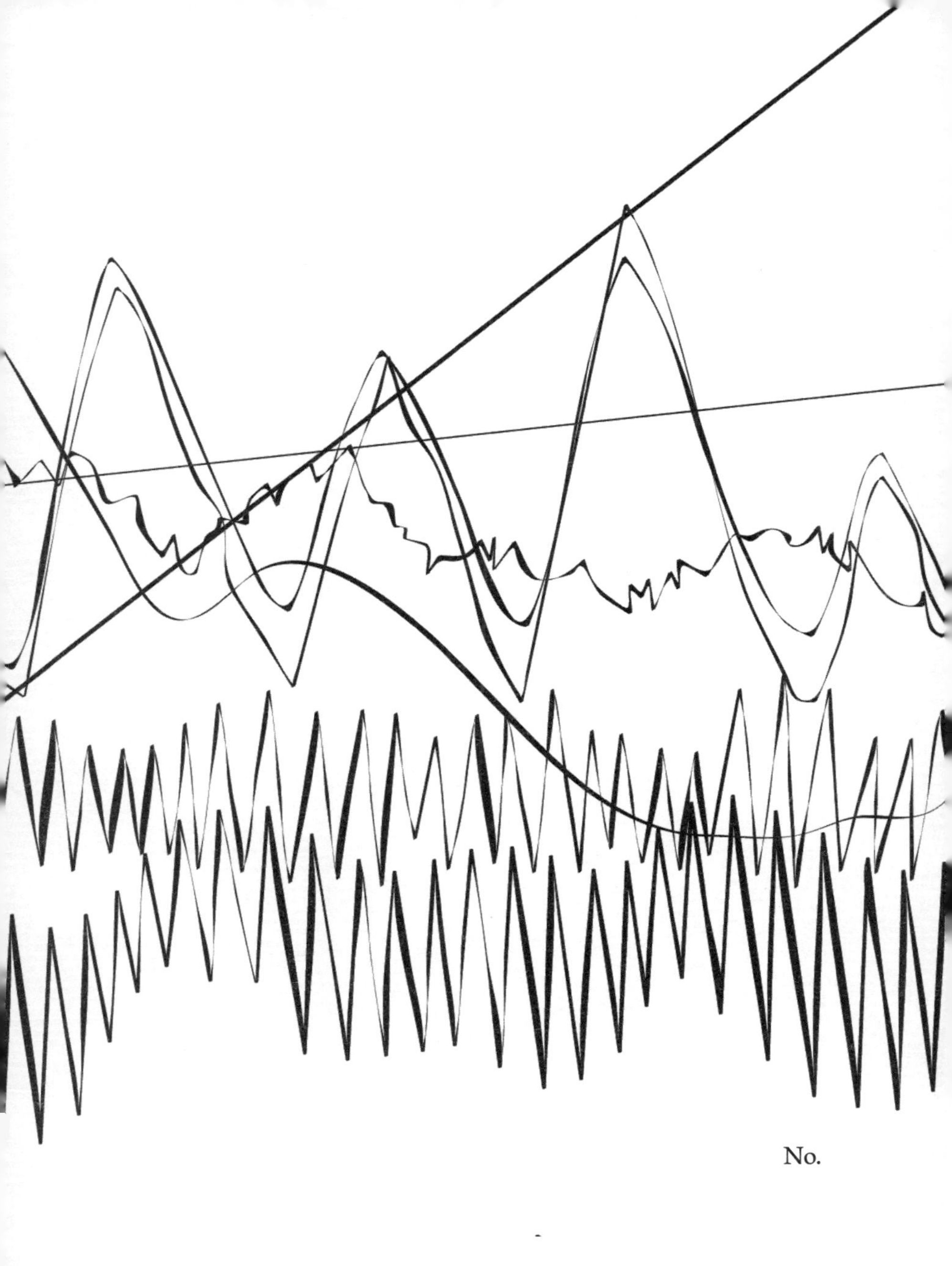

No.

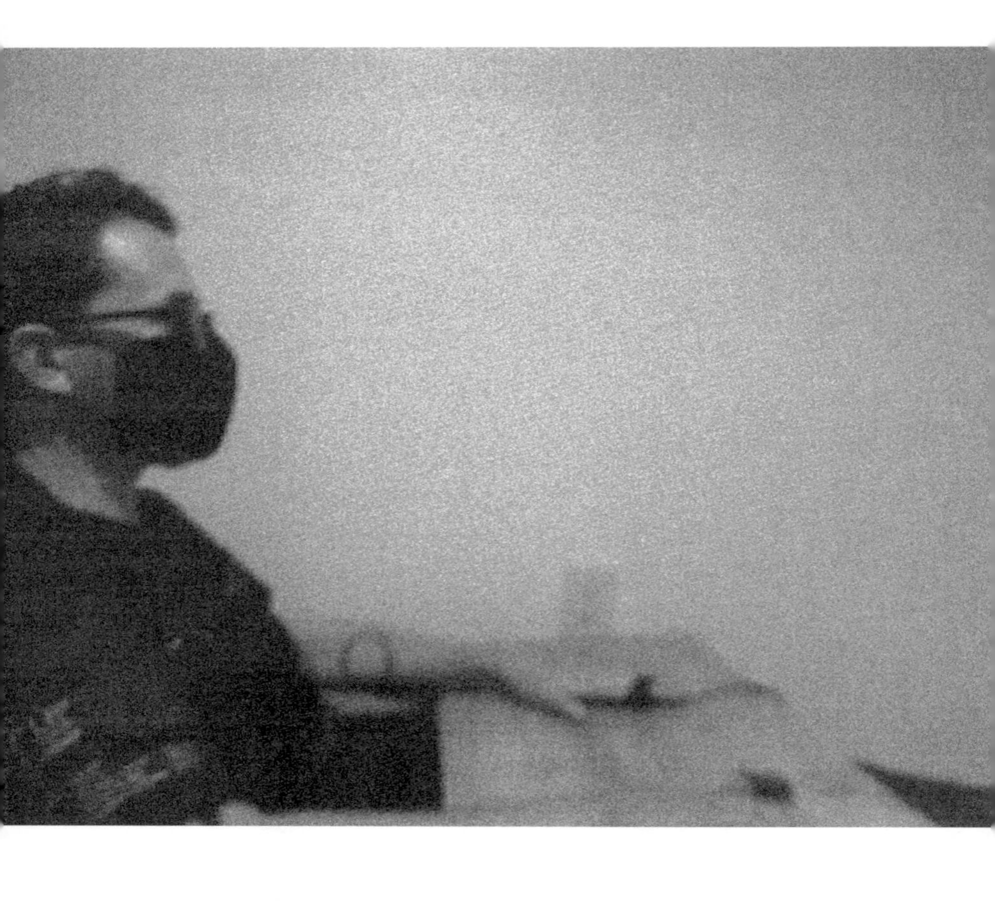

How did that feel?

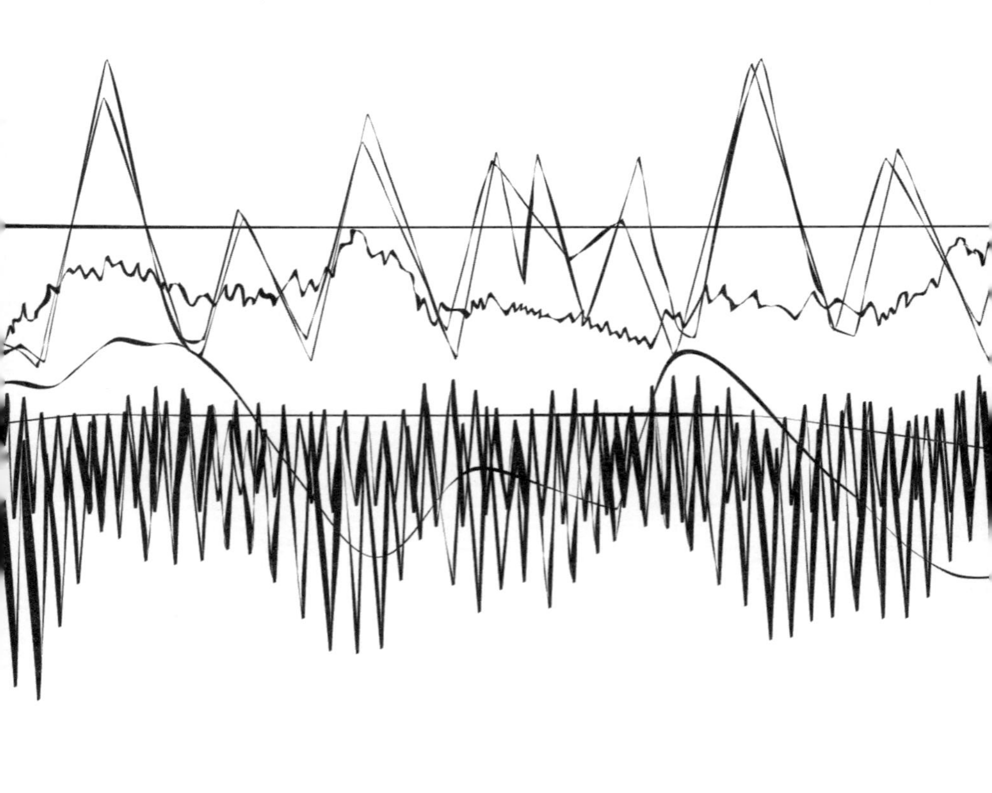

A LIAR

A LINE

A LYRE

'Poets are fakers
Whose faking is so real
They even fake the pain
They truly feel'

– Charles Bernstein, 'Autopsychographia'

We're going to focus on some background questions. This part of the session ensures that you are able to speak truthfully and that you are mentally and physically fit to proceed with the polygraph test today.

Please answer the following questions truthfully.

Where are you from?

He sits upright and orients his gaze toward the camera.

after the fullness of night / I arrived at the border / he eyed the length
of my surname / a distance I could never travel

there / he saw the lines of kin / 'how do you pronounce your last name?'
he asked / 'did your family change it?' / this is where I found myself

lost / my tongue lolled at its limit / unsettling the certainty of living it /
a line crossing a line / struck / I forced it through my teeth & stuttered
the revelatory cut

I was sighed into a palimpsest / photographs with no names / a map
with lines faint / my family's uncertain phrase

we were not taught to look too deeply at the tangle of roots / just the
finger pointing to the tree / I open its file & see the error line

I could retrace my westward steps / to run my finger in the once
nomadic / only to settle again along these same waterways / taught
to shrug longingly whenever asked

How would you describe your childhood?

He positions his hands across his lap. He orients his gaze away from the camera.

of their territory
of this Niagara fruit & farmland
of constant careful work
of oats & barley & grain
of basement-shelved quarts
of weeds & leaves
of chicks & lambs
of colts & calves
of mink / full of life
of pelt preparation

of city & country
of the plant
of the timeclock
of strike lines & pickets
of policy & paycheques
of schoolwork
of the relief from school / &
of waiting for school again
of laughter & a smile
of discipline to the family

of the wild / the north
of the robin & all the birds
of the Opikinemikima shore
of coins & arrowheads
of brush wolves & coyotes
of the art of trapping
of the hunt & the fear
of being hunted
of the truest types of Canadians
of getting all they loved

of telling & listening to stories
of the legend they have made

in love / my grandfather & my

grandmother / knit their house

of three worlds / hemmed by open

fields / I remember once standing

at its back / among our

bloodlines & threads / listening

to speeches that lined their love &

sewed my grandparents as one /

the patchwork of their dream / that

gave them their loving boys /

that recounted my grandmother

who wore an old shirt / on which

she stitched / with heartfelt

feeling / the words marg

loves bert / that did not recount

that my grandfather / a merchant

marine / tattooed upon his forearm /

in a faint blue heart / the name maria

How long have you lived in the city? Do you like it?

He rotates his head to the right. He lowers his right hand to his thigh. He extends his fingers. He orients his gaze toward the camera.

contemplate all the dreams that bring you to this city / of all the cities in the world / think of everything you hope to love & to learn there / everyone / everything / consider the unspoken lines & possibility's promise / when you arrive / remember that the water is always there for you / see all of this on its horizon / do this for ten years

contemplate everyone you abandoned / everyone you are no longer present for / see them all on the horizon / think of your mother / your grandmother / maybe your father / then think of your friends / consider that you may see them again but learn slowly that you never will / lay gently down your hands / trace the traffic lines across your chest / do this for ten years

Describe your relationship with your mother.

He clutches his hands and orients his gaze away from the camera.

cardboard boxes obscure the
curio cabinet in our basement

for as long as we've lived
there / the cabinet has been

unopened / the boxes unmoved
in the 1970s / she wrote

to pen pals from teen magazines / a
self she hardly recalls / she shrugs

when asked / 'that's what we did
in those days' / days that have dissolved

in my lasting presence / I wonder
if she imagines the language

of those letters that landed in the soft
hands of a now-nameless

someone / but if I peek past the basement's
cardboard stacks / the cabinet's dusted

panes / I glimpse small piles of unsealed
letters / fans of joined bamboo / photographed

women / & figures plastic-wrapped while
dusty hanbok hang in the closet upstairs

How often do you eat?

He lifts his left hand to his jaw. He touches his mandible.
He tilts his head.

gradually impress yourselves upon my body / generously rub it with fat & salt / then pass me to another / who will rest their hands

to moan / repeat until sufficient / slice open the body / caesarian / like a crack in my mother's closet door / upstairs where you may whisper your apologies or

you may lay down your petty sorrows / leave the flaps intact so you may close the belly when you're done but leave it open for as long as you need / in its interior

/ stuff with time / press your longings & excesses / your regret / place your memories & your memory's memories / salt generously this wound

/ then / pass it to another / who has busied their hands with the bare ceramic / precisely weighing & preparing the other enumerations that edify this body

when sufficient / seal the belly flap & place my body onto the grill / let me cook until I say I'm done & wander away / & let me recall your words

/ how you said / I love you / while you longed for other bodies

Describe your relationship with your father.

He places his hands in his lap and rubs his palms. He orients his gaze away from the camera.

as she speaks / my father is sitting in a hospital room / a semblance of my blood & roots / his body in wires / elsewhere / but not so far away / & yet / it's a distance I've barely wandered / in sickness / his body is written upon a screen in hooks & bows / lines he's tried to curve all his life / his body needs to be written / written so that we can know its force / so he stares at the wall / his body laid over by a sheet that bares

how many times have you told your heart to beat today?

as she speaks / I am sitting in a room / looking for my semblance in blood / sweat & pulse / my body in wires / elsewhere / but not so far away / but yet / it's a distance I've never travelled / in health / I write my body upon a screen in hooks & bows / lines only now I know I've wanted / my body needn't be written but is written to know what lies beneath / I stare at the wall / sitting in this strange tandem / waiting for the line to write me bare

Who was the disciplinarian in your childhood?

He tilts his head upward and clasps his hands.
He exhales.

while we dreamed / he
worked / while he
dreamed / we wanted as

as children would want / he
was once so loquacious that his
jobs were left undone / lips

so restless that they sentenced
him to the silence of night's shift

in daylight hours / no carpet could soften
our steps / no rule could truly
make us mute / so we lived
in fear of his stir / we felt
it upon our vocal folds / reticence

at the throat / forming under
silence's weight / learning to speak
in timid tongues / just as

I speak now / in the quiet of these lines

Do you ascribe to a particular religion?

He clasps his hands in his lap. He maintains a stationary position.

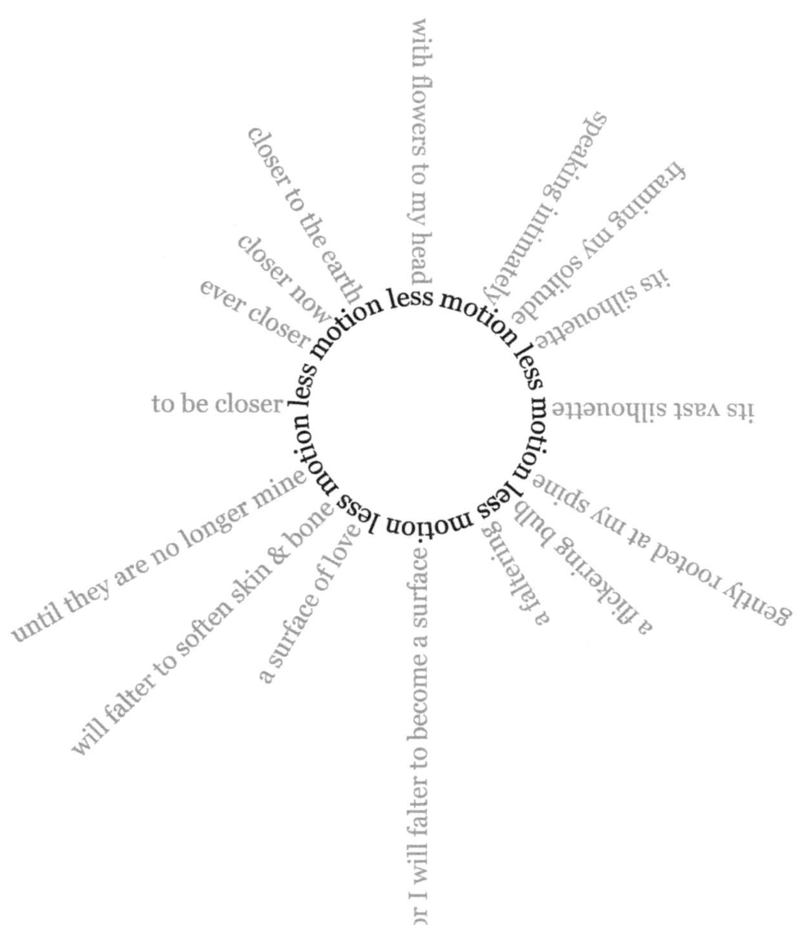
motion less motion less motion less motion less motion less
with flowers to my head
speaking intimately
framing my solitude
its silhouette
its vast silhouette
gently rooted at my spine
a flickering bulb
a faltering
for I will falter to become a surface
a surface of love
will falter to soften skin & bone
until they are no longer mine
to be closer
ever closer
closer now
closer to the earth

Describe your relationship with your siblings if you have any.

He adjusts his hands and orients his gaze away from the camera.
He inhales.

we reach now for small words / of importance / with voices like the winter's wind through our

doorway / where / few memories idle in the cul-de-sac / few twigs crack underfoot / few steps that falsely echo

as they once turned away / I wonder if we counted the memories / if we might enumerate more than our

hands hold now / like the haunting of a snapped bone / cast from on high / or the descent of that decisive chair

if only then / as I can now / feel the impact travelling to our roots / falling like a line from a young bird's song upward from the nest

What does family mean to you?

He rests his right hand on his thigh and adjusts his mask.

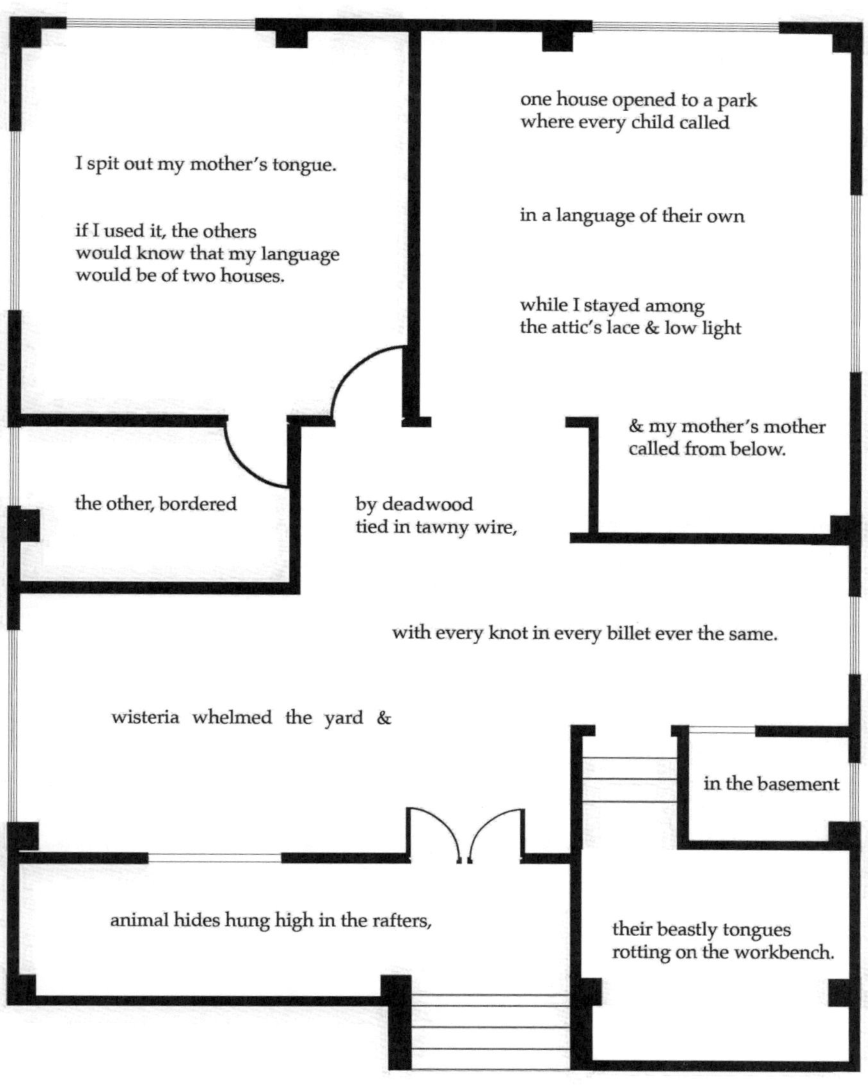
one house opened to a park
where every child called
I spit out my mother's tongue.
in a language of their own
if I used it, the others
would know that my language
would be of two houses.
while I stayed among
the attic's lace & low light
& my mother's mother
called from below.
the other, bordered
by deadwood
tied in tawny wire,
with every knot in every billet ever the same.
wisteria whelmed the yard &
in the basement
animal hides hung high in the rafters,
their beastly tongues
rotting on the workbench.

Describe your relationship with your partner.

He lifts his head and orients his gaze toward the camera.

I look for you like a mushroom peering
through soil & new earthly shades / I

find you at the riverside & I give you
a golden melon that I grew just last spring / I

tuck your book into the bottom of my
bookcase & walk by softly each day / I

place stones on the windowsill so a rainbow
falls upon your face in sunlight / I

photograph the dapple of moonlight across
the kitchen table as you lay out our meal / I

sit next to you as a lover / creating
a silence that never existed / I

write you these words / this poem I write /
these words / a poem / I write for you

Can you describe a time when you felt your worst?

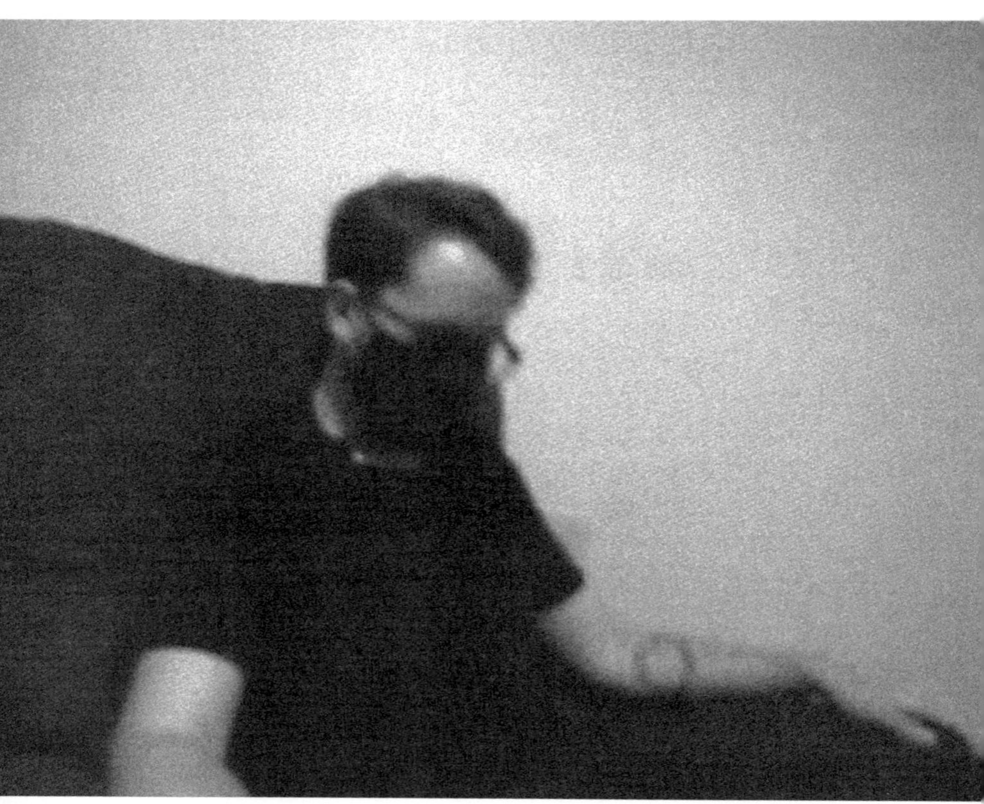

He ceases movement. He lowers his head and exhales.

I passed / thru the front door & into a perceptible breeze / I could sense the end / in its aromatics / as it is beginning on my tongue & lungs / I stepped into the connotation / of a flame as it brought forth / the warmth of all things / I remember the radiant earth / at the fork in the park's path & the woman / who sobs / on the bench / looking to the field of grass / I realize that these words are of pollen & ash

Can you describe a time when you felt your best?

He orients his gaze away from the camera. He gestures with his hands.

flame / pollen & ash / are of my words / these / that realize I / of I / as passed / lungs to a tongue / I who sobs forth I / into its beginning & into end / in the field of all things / I could sense & remember / the warmth on a front door / thru it / the connotation of the grass / & woman looking at the fork in the park's stepped path / the bench / the aromatics brought on the breeze / the perceptible radiant earth / as it is

How would you describe yourself?

I was born / was born & raised / born & grew up / I am the youngest child / the eldest / the middle child / I am the only girl amongst five brothers / the only boy among four girls / I am the only boy / the only girl / my family moved when I was a child / moved when I was a teenager / my family returned before I was ten / didn't return / I have attended / I have graduated / graduated with honours / I have been a proud recipient /

I am a cherished brother / a cherished mother / I am a mother / I am a dear father / a beloved father / a loving father / a loving mother / a loving & supportive mother / I am a dear dad / I am a beloved husband / I am a proud father / a proud mother / a very proud grandfather / my grandchildren are the joy of my life / my nieces & my nephews are the joy of my life / I have lifelong friends who add so much to my life / & I love them deeply /

I have earned / I have spent / I have served / served & trained / served for many years / I have been a proud member / I have made / made home / I have demonstrated / I have played / I have joined / I have worked / worked long & hard / industriously & long / for many years / until retirement / not one to sit idle / I have laughed / I have embarked / I have returned / I have balanced / I have managed / I have loved / I have been loved / I have sacrificed much / I became /

I am passionate / I am warm & generous / I have zest for life / I am ambitious & determined / I have an adventurous spirit / I am elegant & stylish / I am avid / I am an accomplished artist / a true gourmet / a talented chef / & an eager photographer / I love to host in my home with music & laughter / I love to laugh / I care deeply for those around me / I am always ready to help / I see the best in everyone / & I always speak words of encouragement & kindness / I am selfless & kind to all those who have the honour of crossing paths with me / I am an inspiration to all who know me / I am an honest & generous man / I have a true word for everyone I meet /

I will die / I will die suddenly / unexpectedly / quietly / I will pass away / pass away in my sleep / peacefully / hearts will be broken / hearts will grieve / hearts will be heavy / it will be announced with deepest sorrow / it will be tearfully said /

I will be remembered / lovingly remembered / fondly remembered / I will be remembered for my kindness / love / & dedication / I will be remembered as a beautiful woman / inside & out / I will be missed / will be dearly missed / deeply missed / will be greatly missed / I am predeceased / I am survived /

friends & relatives will be invited / a memorial service will be held / a funeral service will be held / a celebration of life will be held / friends & family will be received / many thanks will be given / expressions of sympathy will be made / donations will be given in my honour / wishes will be kept / you will be asked to take a moment to hug a loved one / to walk in nature / watch a sunset / or appreciate the beauty & scent of a delicate bloom / my remains will be spread / my memory will live on in the hearts of all who knew me / a tree will be planted in my honour / & in that tree / my memory will lie

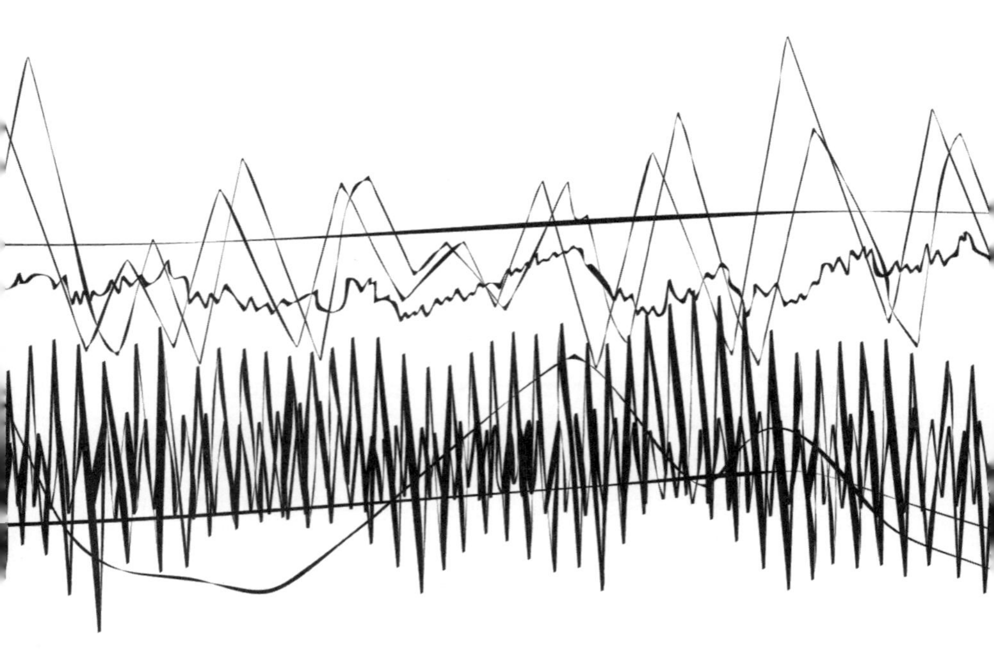

A LIAR

A LINE

A LYRE

'Intimacy is not just about getting "in touch" with our inner selves; it also turns us inside out.'

– Sun-ha Hong, *Technologies of Speculation*

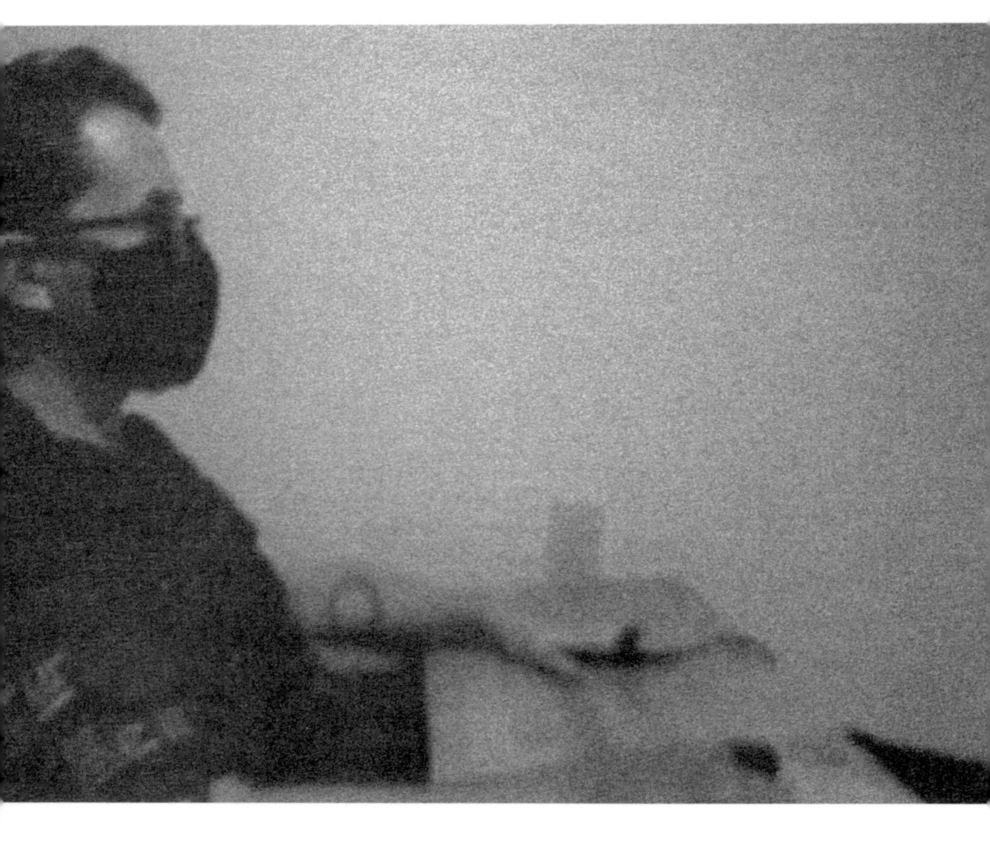

Remember, you can be as nervous as you like. Nervousness and deception look different.

Do not move. Tell me when you would like to begin.

I am increasing the blood-pressure cuff. This test is about to begin. Please sit quietly and answer only with yes or no questions. Do you understand that? I will only be asking questions we have reviewed regarding ████. Do you intend to answer truthfully?

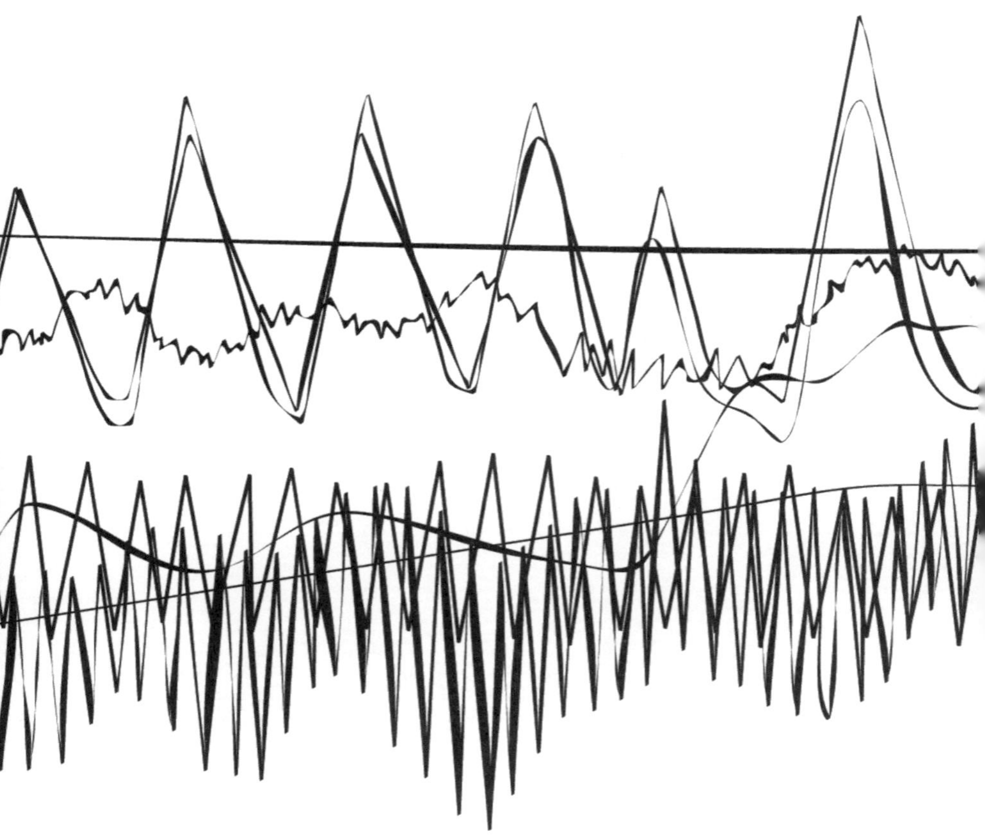

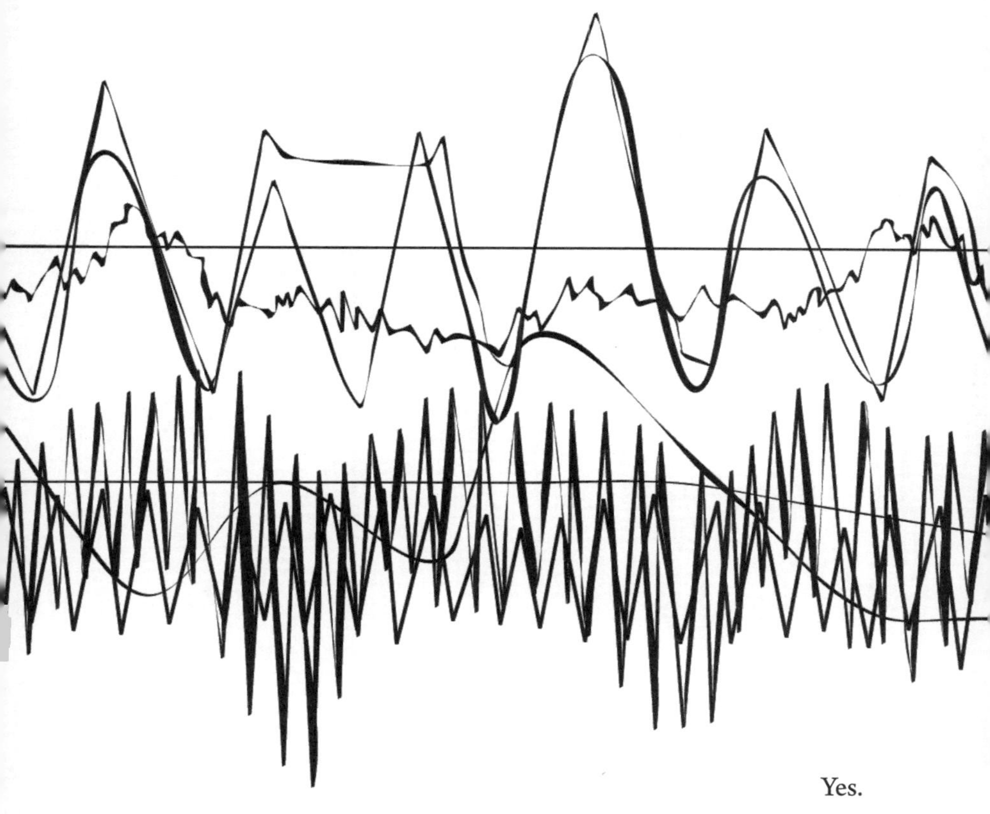

Yes.

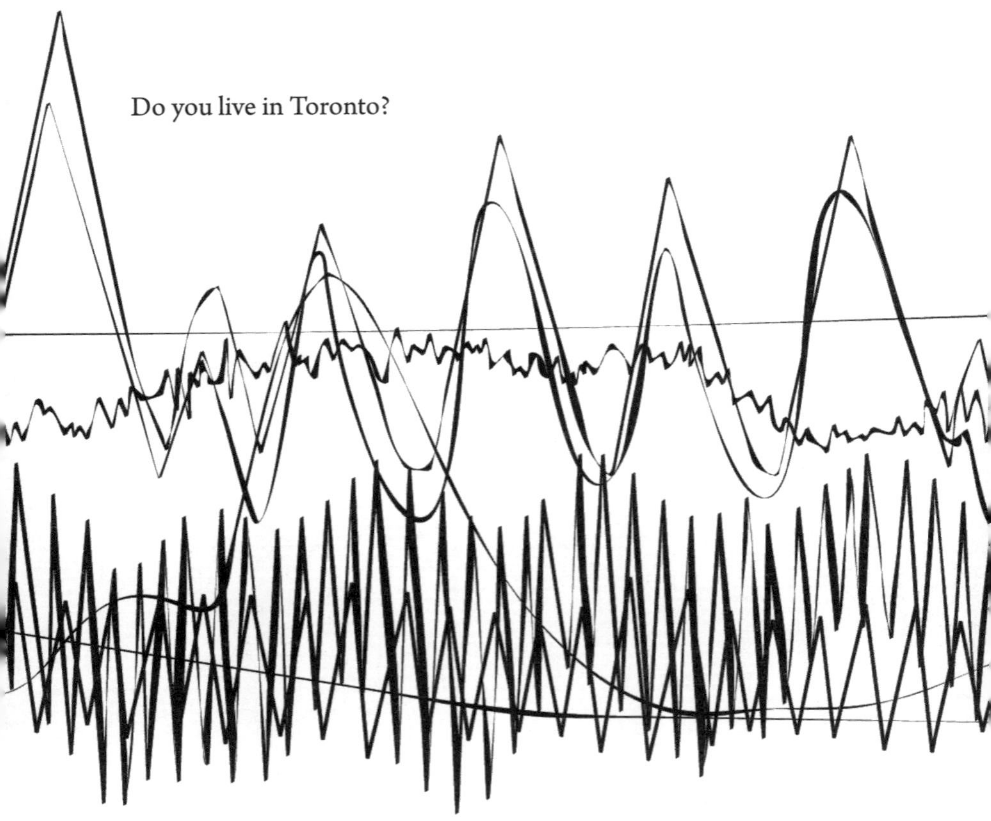

Do you live in Toronto?

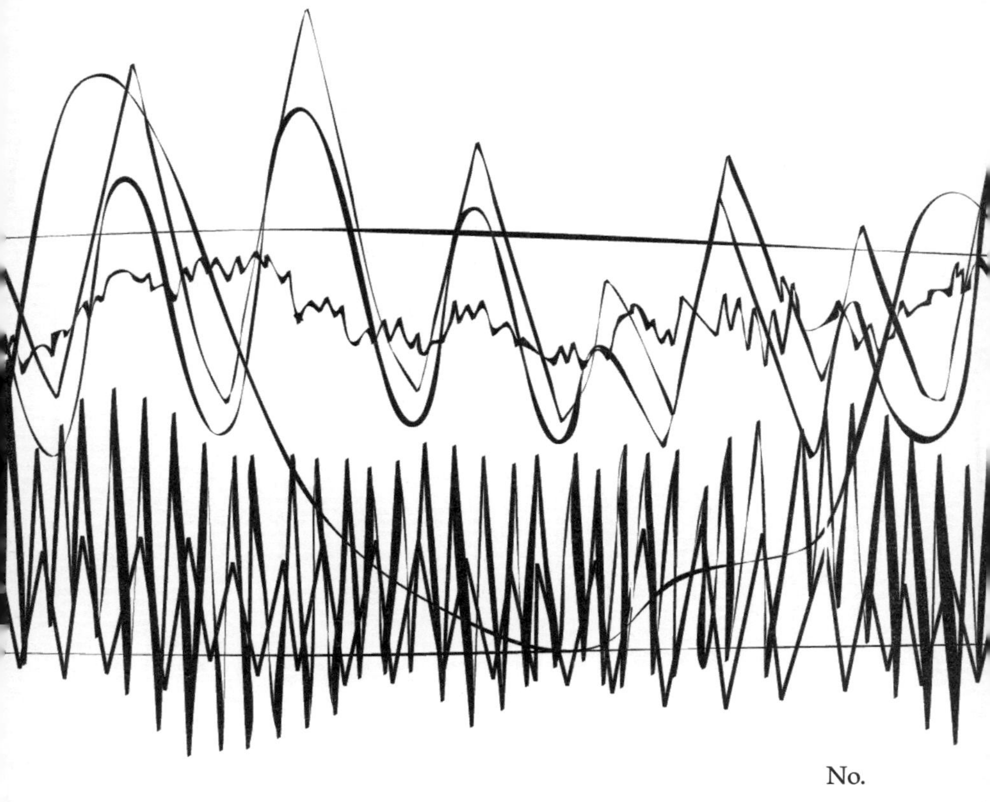

No.

Have you ever ████ from ████ ████ that you have ████ from other ████ or ████?

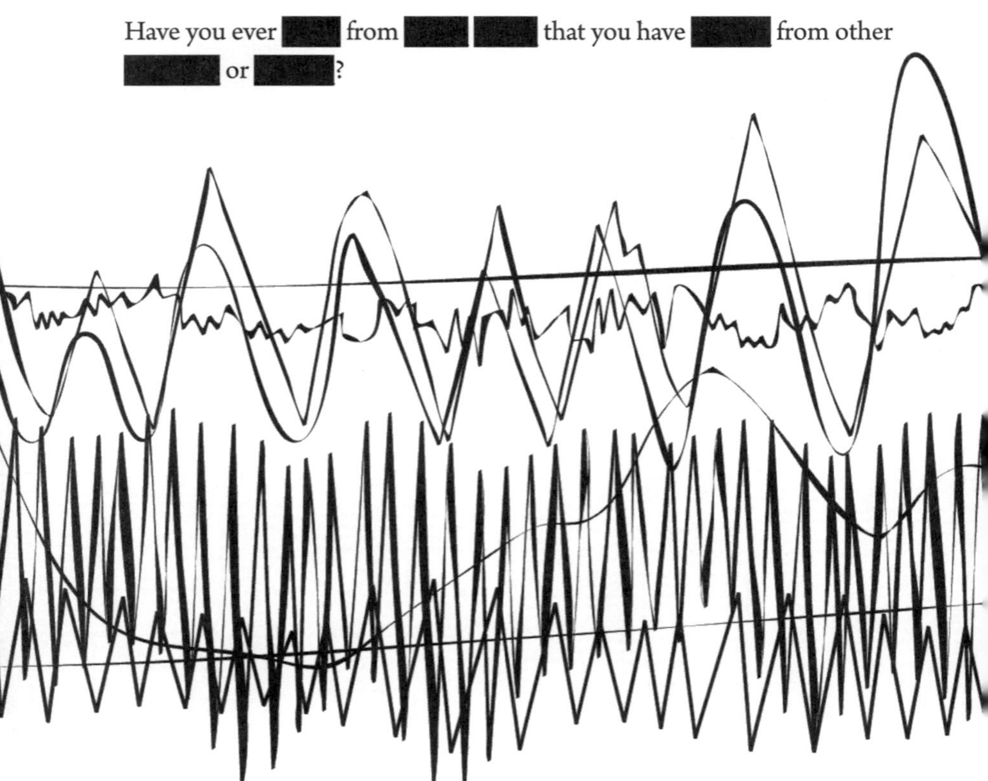

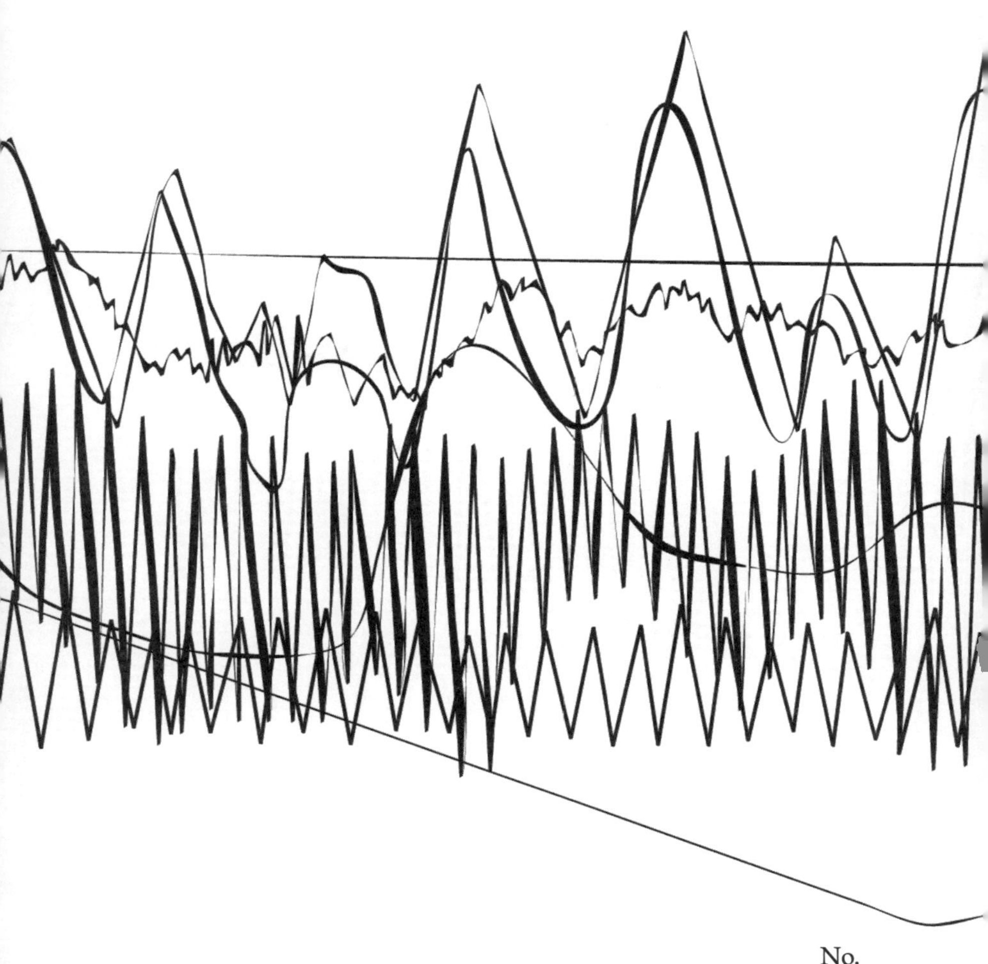

No.

Did you intentionally ████ ████ in the last twenty-four hours?

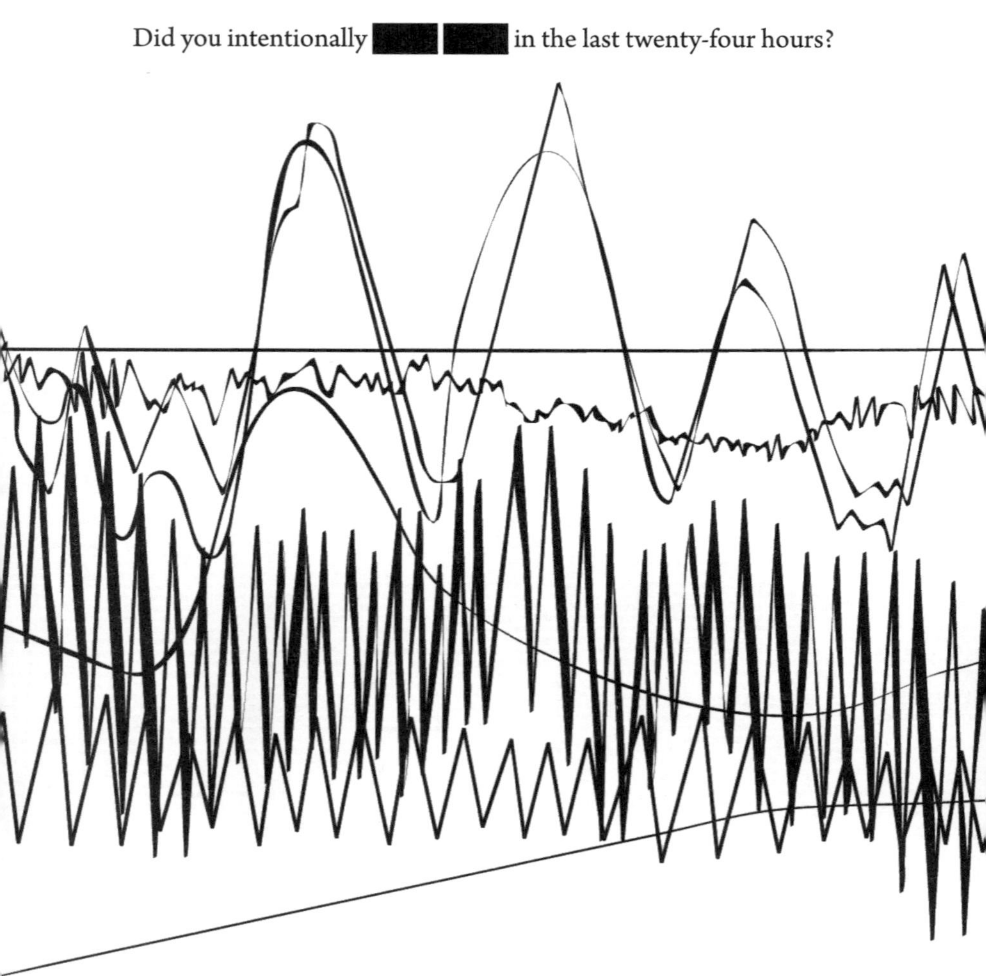

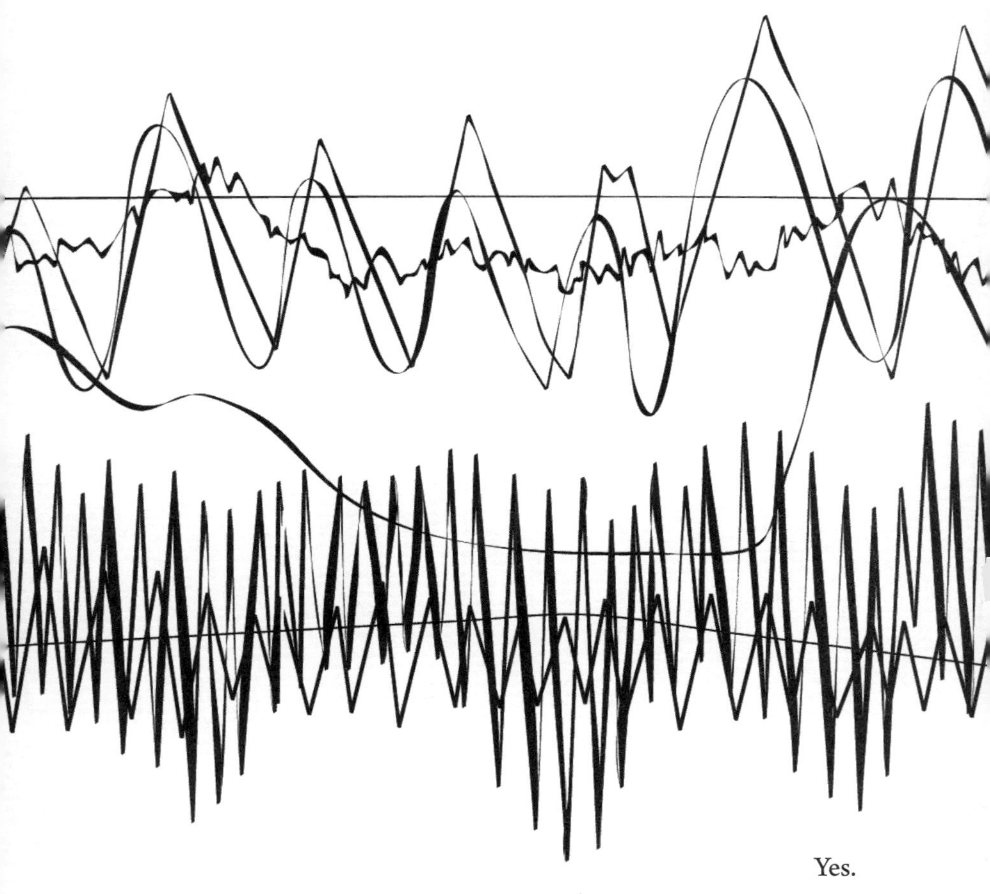

Yes.

Did you make up any part of ███ ████?

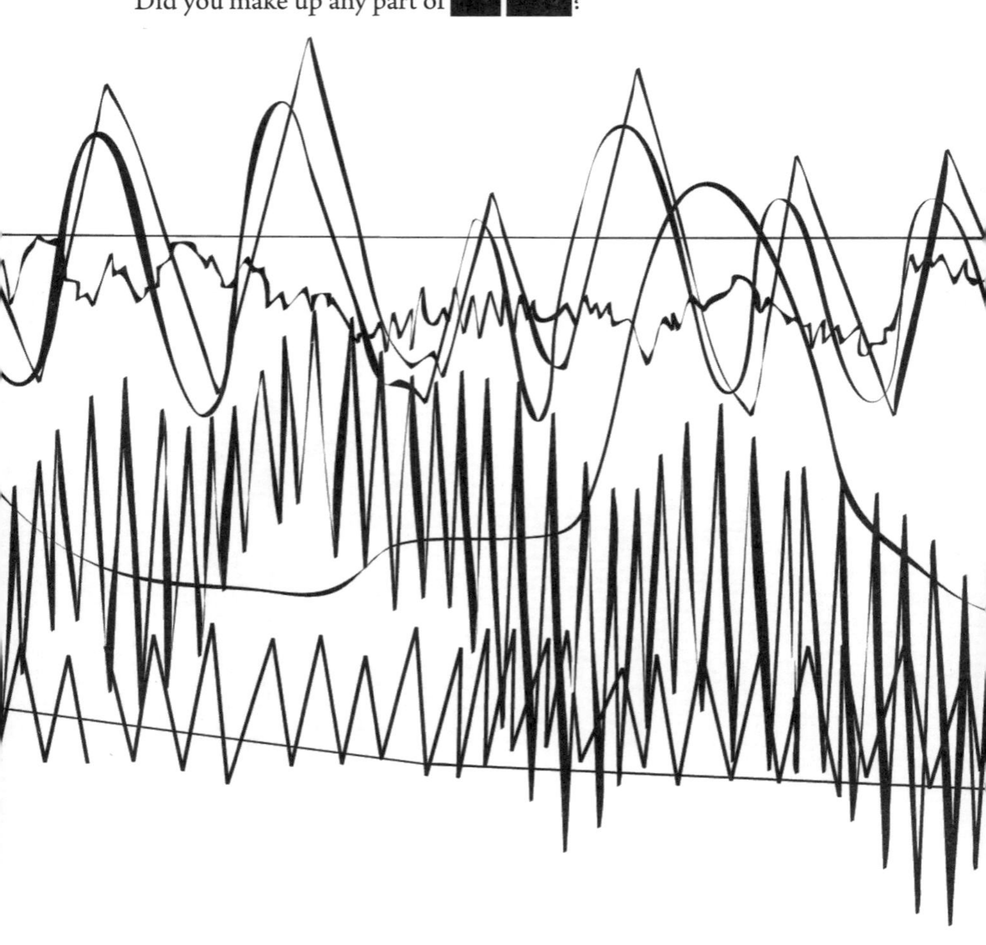

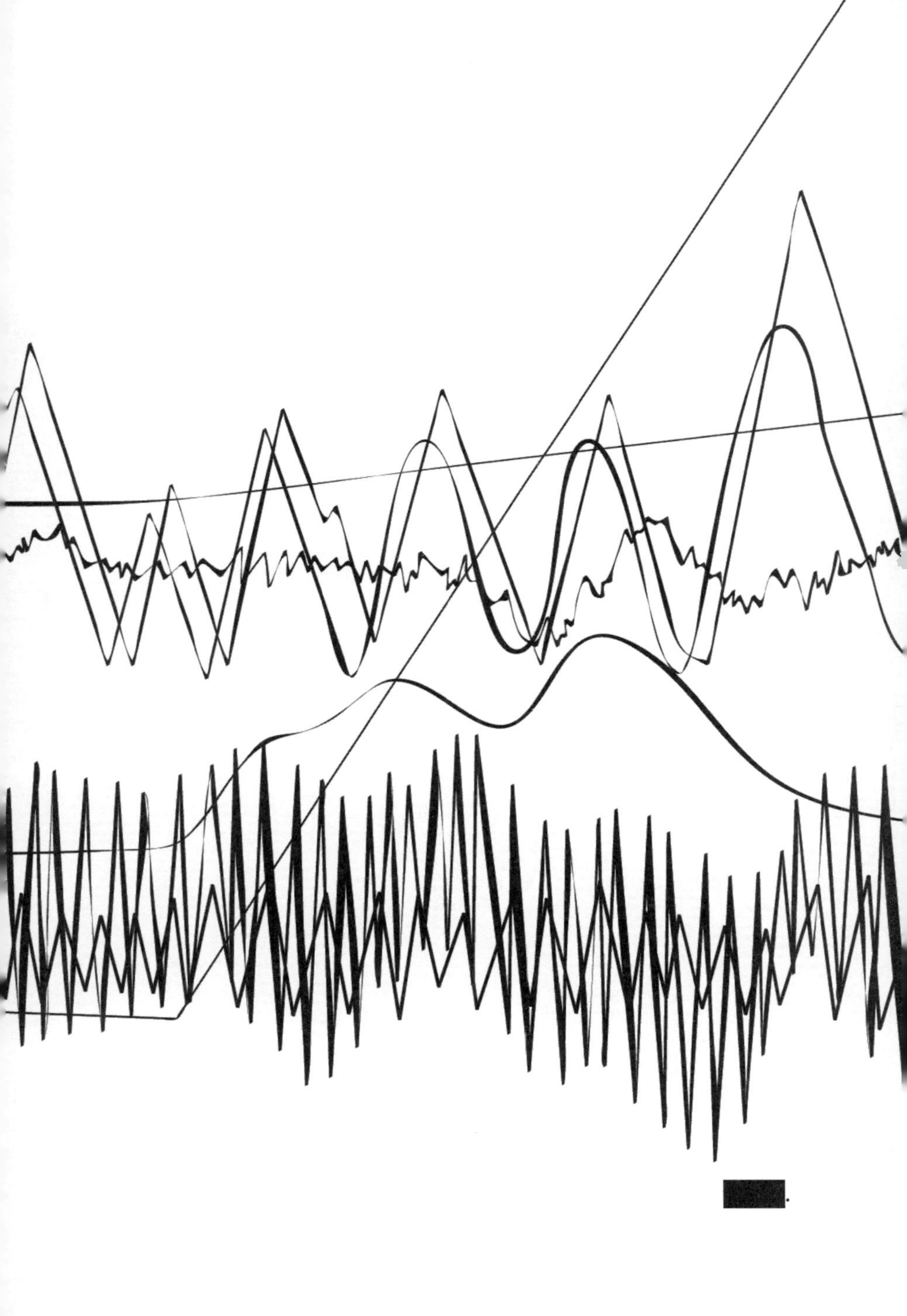

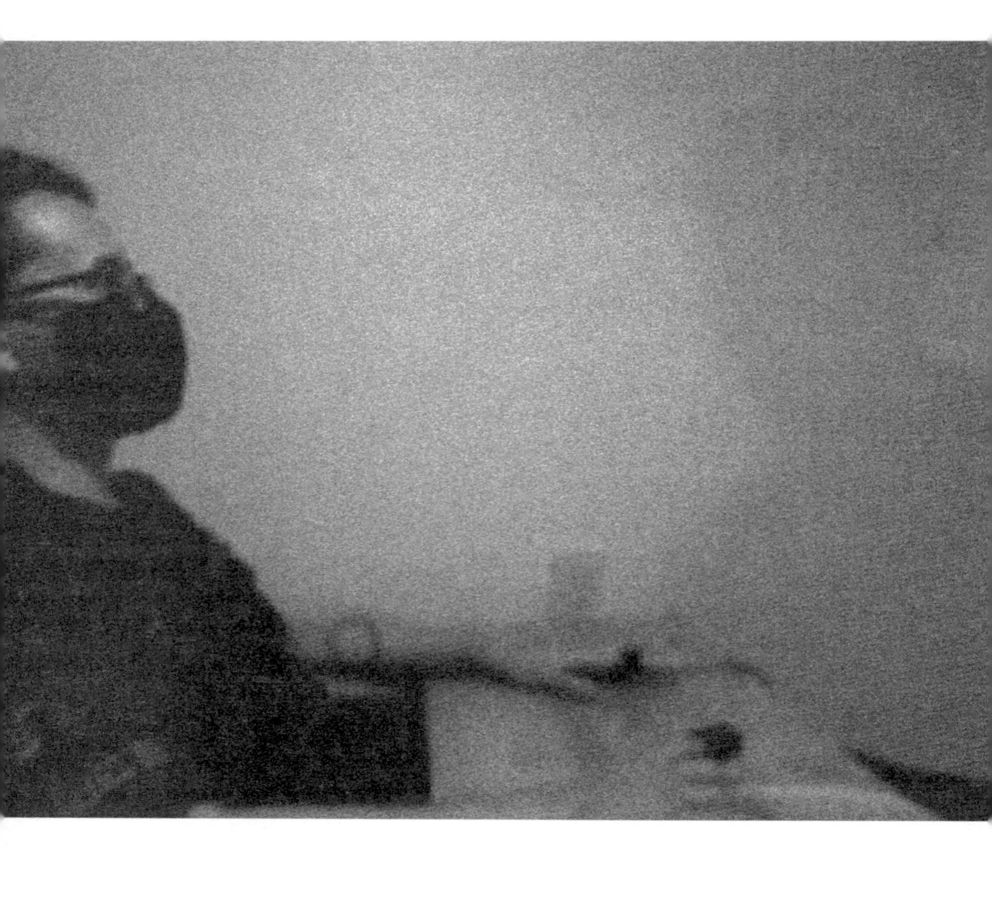

Emily Cauduro, Polygraph Specialist

Dear Eric Schmaltz,

Re: Polygraph Examination

I have provided a letter documenting the findings of the polygraph examination that was administered to you at my office on , , , at : a.m.

The purpose of the polygraph test was to determine whether you have ever during your time .

Testing was conducted using the computerized polygraph instrument that monitors and records data related to physiological changes and motion.

The charts were scored using the guidelines of the American Polygraph Association (APA) and the Canadian Association of Police Polygraphers (CAPP). Their criteria are supported by research and employed by accredited polygraph schools in Canada and the United States.

After manually interpreting the polygraph charts and confirming the raw data, your numerical score was tabulated in the range.

Following the polygraph examination, secondary test analysis of all physiological channels was completed by way of a computerized algorithm. The findings were consistent with the examiner's scores where there was also to the relevant questions.

To conclude, the test was deemed ██ ████████ ████ based on ██ ██████ reactions to the relevant questions. It is in the opinion of this examiner that Eric was ██████ ███ ████ on this examination.

Please note: While the polygraph is a useful investigative tool that statistically provides a high degree of accuracy in relation to the probability of truthfulness and/or deception, it is not 100% accurate, and therefore fallible. Clients are encouraged to consider polygraph results in context with all other available and pertinent information.

Yours Truly,

Emily Cauduro, M.Sc., B.Sc.

Afterword

by Orchid Tierney

Eric Schmaltz declares 'I confess' – but what exactly is the Poet confessing to? The Poet's utterances evoke the resonances of a possible crime, a spiritual sin, or a moral transgression; and yet at no point do the poems articulate their responsibility for whatever misdeed they have performed. At stake in *I Confess*, however, is not the supposed transgression itself – whatever it may be – but the shifting states of 'the truth' and its counterpart, 'the deception.' The lyrical poems in this collection are catalogues that organize the aura of veracity that one's memories, positionality, and subjectivity constantly reform over time. And if this collection serves to explore the elusive elements of poetic truth, then the Poet reveals the difficult strangeness of this goal, this *thing*, this *charge* for the lyrical subject, who finds himself embedded in an ecosystem of affect and identity. We, as readers, must grapple with the realization that poetic truth cannot be affixed to a single idea, axiom, category, or fact. Indeed, *I Confess* destabilizes any quest for universal, absolute, and scientific Truth. These binaries of veracity and falsehood collapse under the duress of the poet's self-investigations. As Schmaltz writes at the beginning of this collection: 'Some of what you will read is true; the rest is poetry.' And so: if Schmaltz is on trial, in a confession box, or sitting on the polygrapher's chair, then we – the readers – are not his judge and executioner but interpreters of his assertions.

In truth, I was surprised to learn that I was a witness to this collection's inception. As I prepared to write this afterword, Schmaltz reminded me in a Zoom meeting that the foundations for *I Confess* had been laid at a Poetry and Poetics event, comprised of graduate students and faculty, at the University of Pennsylvania in 2018. I vaguely recall that a small group of us had gathered to discuss his then-recently published book *Surfaces*. If I am to accept Schmaltz's version of this event, I (allegedly) asked him whose body was represented in that particular book. In all honesty, I remember this discussion somewhat differently; I believe it was either Davy Knittle or Charles Bernstein (and I'm *mostly* sure it was the latter) actually posed this question. But in the context of my confession and Schmaltz's *I Confess*, does the veracity of this moment really matter? The failure of our collective memory of this event underscores the fragile constructions of the truth and its expressions in the book. What matters is that truth is really a partial thing, but the robustness of the lyrical poem can hold these ambiguities with grace, even if the documented record skips it. Such grace is inherent in the pleasure of poetic form and in the indeterminateness of memory that underlies Schmaltz's verse in *I Confess*. Michael Donaghy may call the poem a 'diagram of consciousness,' but Schmaltz's poems are a forensic study into truth's mystification.

TECHNOLOGIES OF TRUTH-MAKING

'chlorinated & sodden I sunk / to the bottom of the pool,' writes the Poet. Medieval modes of determining the truth of any statement made by a criminal defendant, moral deviant, or heretic typically relied upon the violent execution of painful 'trials of ordeals' upon the vulnerable body. These trials – of combat, fire, and cold water, which Schmaltz explores in the first section of *I Confess* – subjected the body to extreme physical and psychological torture to bring the defendant, deviant, or heretic into a closer relationship with the truth and to God. These barbaric methodologies for determining veracity now appear antiquated and uncivilized. When Schmaltz stages these violent truth-extraction methods alongside their modern iterations of waterboarding, truth serums, forensic photography, and polygraphy, we must question whether our own modern technologies are not also imbued with the elements of the painful sublime. The viciousness of truth extraction is evident in *I Confess*. We, too, become involved in Schmaltz's ordeal as willing witnesses; we affix our gaze upon the unnerved, discomforted, and frightened subject. And I must ask: How really different is an ordeal of cold water from the ordeal of the polygraph? Are we complicit in this theatre of truth-extraction? Is this poetry or the truth?

Truth telling requires the participation of at least two actors: the speaker of a statement or, in this collection's case, the poem, and the listener or reader, who witnesses the utterance. But in *I Confess,* we also encounter other agents in this social arrangement: the mechanisms of documentation – such as the camera and polygraph machine – and the polygrapher, whose task is to interpret the data inscriptions of the tests. The polygraph charts in *I Confess* foreground a novel writing practice, whereby the body's expulsions of sweat, gesture, respiration, and heart rhythms are extracted from the test subject and registered as embodied language. In this sense, Schmaltz introduces us to an astonishingly expanded field of poetry beyond recognizable semantics to identify the non-verbal context clues that are integral to the production of meaning. Schmaltz asks us to scrutinize with intensive exuberance his body and behaviours, to observe his subtle movements, affects, gestures, impressions, and nervousness as part of this poetic inscription. Far from being supplemental, the polygraph charts, the gestural descriptions, and the photograph *are* the poems in *I Confess.* They have to be, because everything else just might be the truth.

Polygraphy involves different vectors for documenting how truthful a subject is when they respond to a question. The examiner reads the amplitude, duration, and frequency of the signals, and compares these elements with baseline and relevant responses. These initial baseline questions will have known answers (such as 'Is your name Eric Schmaltz?' or 'Do you live in Toronto?') and will establish the physiological responses to deceptive and nondeceptive answers. The examiner will compare these baseline channel signals with the responses to the relevant questions that follow. The actual polygraph chart is comprised of three channels: the pneumograph channel, which captures respiratory patterns; the cardiograph channel, which records heart rate and blood pressure; and the galvanic skin response, which measures sweat gland activity. In *I Confess,* the test subject is also observed for behaviours that might indicate their physiological response to the examiner's questions.

Clearly polygraphy holds incredible sway as a representation of the Truth – with a capital T – in popular culture. Consider how this device – also known as a lie detector test in common parlance – appears frequently in criminal television dramas as an actor that can singularly condemn or exonerate a character. Yet in actuality, polygraphy is, at best, a pseudoscience that relies upon the mailable interpretations of an examiner, whose positionality, like the Poet's, is never value-neutral. Indeed, the tests are not 100 percent accurate, as the examiner reminds Schmaltz. Instead, we might attend to how the photographs and the polygraph charts in *I Confess* reframe the Poet as both a willing *and* slightly reluctant 'test subject.' Here, the body of the Poet endures the awkward arrangement of the polygrapher's wires and electrodes at the same time he is subjected to the cool gaze of the camera. This body is clearly under pressure as it becomes a thing to be written upon: 'my tongue lolled at its limit,' the Poet writes, 'unsettling the certainty of living it / a line crossing a line / struck / I forced it through my teeth & stuttered the revelatory cut.' The body is not only a lab rat in these experiments but the Poet also becomes the medium for his poems. It's natural then when we examine the photographs and read the polygraph charts, we search for evidence of how this ordeal marks this vulnerable body. Like the polygraph examiner, I, too, want to know the answer to the question 'How did it feel?' I want to hear the truth.

POEM-AS-POLYGRAPH

Schmaltz notes in his poem 'Trial by Voice' that 'The truth peaks while lies plateau.' If the polygraph is not an accurate tool, then what does it mean to consider the lyrical poem, its lines and line-endings, as a chart for some kind of truth. Here, the lyrical 'I' must be dissected in the lines of the poem just as we dissect the the lines of the polygraphy chart. In many respects, it is Schmaltz's lyrical poems that provide us with a vector toward authenticity. His poetic lines become a technology for a *kind of* truth – not *the* Truth, but a truthiness – because the poem is always conditional, situational, and contextual. And perhaps that's the whole truth of this matter? Schmaltz brilliantly recalls Emily Dickinson's truth-making adage – 'Tell all the Truth but tell it slant,' and in the process, he reminds us that our modern lyrical poem neither makes claims for any spontaneous overflow of powerful feeling, nor does it give us unmitigated access to the Poet's inner emotional world. Rather, when the Poet announces that 'my body needn't be written but is written to know what lies beneath / I stare at the wall … waiting for the line to write me bare,' he underscores the relationality of our bodies to our environs and to language. This idea, I believe, is the point – well, one of them – that *I Confess* is making. In this age of misinformation, disinformation, and political liars who tell us that we cannot trust the scientific registrars of knowledge, that we should discount what we *see* in the photograph or what we *hear* on tape, the poem's strength *lies* in its ability to hold the multiplicities of the self. And when Schmaltz declares his plural selves as figures of familial relation –

> / I am a cherished brother / a cherished mother / I am a mother
> / I am a dear father / a beloved father / a loving father / a loving
> mother / a loving & supportive mother /

– all these identities may be slightly true-*ish* (but they can also be slightly false). This refusal of the Poet to lock his self to any one thing is part of the brilliance of *I Confess*: we are never quite certain what to make of a poem's claims. That's the pleasure of this text. And as Schmaltz suggests: 'my memory will lie.' But even lies will approximate the truth. And that's the whole truth.

Further Confessions

I Confess was imagined first as a provocation. What if, like the lyric poem, I used a device to draw out my most profound feelings, emotions, & utterances? If the poem is an art form that expresses the truth, I wanted to locate the poem within a history of procedures devised to produce the truth. These include trials by ordeal & apocryphal technologies & methods such as the polygraph test – also known as the lie detector. *I Confess* explores truth-telling & subjectivity in its various forms – its violence, vulnerabilities, freedoms, superstitions, & pseudoscience. In its own way, this book tries to speak a truth about the poem & the complexities of truth-telling.

'Performative Utterances' (p. 18) uses two versions of the oath for sworn testimony, both used in courts in the United States. The parallel text comprises various historical forms of truth-telling.

'Trial by Combat' (p. 20) is a meta-ekphrastic poem in that it comprises a series of minimal descriptions of images on the Google image search page I found after searching for the title words of the poem. Notably, alongside a few screenshots from a famous *Game of Thrones* scene, the most frequently repeated image at the time depicted Rudy Giuliani on January 6th calling for a trial by combat at a press conference. Though later explained away as a joke, trial by combat has not been formally abolished in the United States.

'Trial by Touch' (p. 22) is an ekphrastic poem written after I saw a panel from the *Hamburgisches Stadtrecht von 1497* depicting a person undergoing cruentation. This is another trial, primarily for murder trials, that requires the accused to touch the corpse of the dead. If the dead bleed upon touch, the accused is believed to be guilty.

'Trial by Fire' (p. 23) was written after seeing *Peter Igneus Over the Fire*, a painting attributed to Italian painter Marco Palmezzano from the fifteenth century.

'Trial by Force' (p. 24) was created by using language from what is commonly known as the *Wickersham Commission Report* (1931), formally known as *The Report on Lawlessness in Law Enforcement*. The report is regarded as a watershed document in the culture & politics of policing in the United States since it was this report that made violent police interrogations more widely known to the public &, thanks to public pressure, led to reforms in policing methods. This is a found poem, using phrases & words drawn from the report.

'Trial by Voice' (p. 26) was written after learning about an apocryphal method of divining the truth by analyzing soundwaves of speech. Analysts, believing in the validity of this practice, claim that when the truth is spoken the soundwave peaks while a false statement is represented by a plateau.

'Trial by Serum' (p. 28) is a poem about scopolamine, one of numerous so-called 'truth serums' developed in the twentieth century. It is also known as Devil's Breath. Written after Ryan Duffy reported on the drug's use in Colombia for *VICE*.

Water, hot or cold, features prominently in the history of forced truth extraction. 'Trial by Waterboard' (p. 29) draws language from the screenplay for *Zero Dark Thirty* (2011) that involves the words *water* or *ice*. *Zero Dark Thirty*, a controversial film, was criticized by the U.S. Government for its depiction of waterboarding. They claimed they use only 'enhanced interrogation techniques.'

'Trial by Cold Water' (p. 30) was written after I read about cold water ordeals, an early method of determining one's guilt or innocence. It was believed that the guilty would float while the innocent will sink, weighted by their virtue & goodness. This belief has been traced back by medievalist Thomas Hill to the Atlamál, one of the heroic poems of the *Poetic Edda*. I also came across Joseph Kosuth's *Notebook on Water, 1965–66* while writing this poem, which helped deliver it.

'A LIAR' is based on a line of questioning given to me in preparation for a polygraph test I underwent in the late summer of 2021. My answers to these questions would allow my analyst to determine my ability to speak truthfully & to determine my mental & physical fitness before undergoing the actual polygraph test. Having met her only that morning, I found the process deeply unnerving, a kind of therapy I wasn't prepared for. Each poem responds to a question she asked me in the form of a confessional poem, extrapolating from the answers I gave during the session.

Page 55 is a response to a eulogy written by philosopher Dave Goicoechea on the occasion of my grandparents' fiftieth anniversary. Written as a poem, the eulogy is published in a little-known book entitled *Eulogies & Laments* (2003). The left hand column of this poem comprises found text taken from Goichoechea's eulogy, while the right hand column is the response. The poem refers to the 'Opikinemikima shore,' mentioned by Goicoechea in his text. The author has been unable to verify the location of this shore or its existence.

Page 61 was written after Philip Metres' poem 'Recipe from the Abbasid.'

The italicized line in the poem on page 63 was spoken by Emily Cauduro during our disussion regarding polygraph tests.

Page 67 is dedicated to Gerry Shikatani, whose writing appreciates stillness, silence, & meaning in small gestures.

Page 71 was written after reading Kate Siklosi. Thanks to Kate for her encouragement with this poem.

Pages 75 & 77 are cut-ups containing the same words in each poem. I took liberties with the punctuation marks. I dedicate this poem to Gregory Betts, whose anagrams inspired me to write long ago.

Pages 79–81 were written using phrases found in online obituaries for persons with the first name Eric or the last name Schmaltz.

Both sequences of 'A LYRE' are recreations of my actual physiological data as I underwent a polygraph analysis, including representations of my breath, pulse, & perspiration. A third chart is reproduced throughout the book alongside some of the paratext. I dedicate these sequences to Judith Copithorne, who brought body & text into close alignment.

Meaningful Utterances

Research & writing for this book began on the Indigenous land known as Lenapehoking (also known as Philadelphia, Pennsylvania), which is the Indigenous homeland of the Lenape Peoples. From there, this book was composed in the areas known as Tkaronto & on lands that have been taken care of by the Anishinabek Nation, the Haudenosaunee Confederacy, the Huron-Wendat, & the Métis, & the current treaty holders Mississaugas of the Credit First Nation, as well as the Banff area, known as Minhrpa & the Treaty 7 territory, home to the Shuswap Nations, Ktunaxa Nations, & Metis Nation of Alberta, Region 3. Work for this book was completed in Kjipuktuk on the territories of the Mi'kmaw, Wolastoqey, & Peskotomuhkati Peoples.

Thank you to the members of the Poetry & Poetics Group at the Kelly Writers House for responding enthusiastically to the initial provocation that formed the foundation for this book years ago: Michael Martin Shea, India Halstead, Orchid Tierney, Amber Rose Johnson, Davy Knittle, & Knar Gavin.

Thank you to the Banff Centre for Arts and Creativity for the necessary writing time and space provided by the Leighton Studio Residency program. Thanks to friends & companions at the Banff Centre, poets Derek Beaulieu, Maddie Beaulieu, & Bren Simmers, & artists Kellyann Marie Irene, Sean Jena Taal, Russell Banx, Scott Elliott, & Aisha Jamal for reminding me how to be an artist.

I extend a special thanks to my Backster-certified polygraph analyst Emily Cauduro for working with me on this project. Without her knowledge, her commitment to research, creativity, & creation, this book would have never formed. She has my deepest gratitude – truly.

Thank you to friends, readers, & mentors whose distinctive & many forms of support, friendship, teaching, encouragement, & kindness I carry with me every day. Thank you to Aaron Kreuter, Aditya Bahl, Alysha Dawn Puopolo, Adam Dickinson, Amaranth Borsuk, Amy

Leblanc, Anna Veprinska, Andy Weaver, Andrew Faulkner, a.rawlings, Asha Jeffers, Astra Papachristodoulou, Bart Vautour, Benjamin Sieff, bill bissett, Brandon McCarthy, Charles Bernstein, Dani Spinosa, Del Stephen, Divya Victor, Donato Mancini, Erin Wunker, Gary Barwin, Gerry Shikatani, Gregory Betts, Hazel Millar, Holly Melgard, Jason Camlot, Jay Millar, Jay Ritchie, Jesse Pajuäär, Jim Johnstone, Jimmy Cahill, Joakim Norling, Joey Yearous-Algozin, Jonathan Ball, Jo Iani, Joseph Mosconi, Kaie Kellough, Kate Siklosi, Kirby, Kyle Flemmer, Lauren Fournier, Leigh Nash, Marc Couroux, Martine Tchitche, Mat Laporte, M.C. Hyland, Michael Nardone, MLA Chernoff, Moez Surani, Myra Bloom, my therapist, Paul Dutton, Paul MacKay, Paul Vermeersch, Petra Schulze-Wollgast, Philip A. Miletic, rob mclennan, Sal Nunkachov, Stephanie Domet, Stephen Cain, the Sangha at the Toronto Zen Centre, Vannessa Barnier, & Zane Koss.

Earlier versions 'A LYRE' appeared as part of a broadside installation series for the 2022 Fertile Festival. Poems from 'A LINE' & 'A LIAR' were performed at Knife Fork Book @ Capital Espresso, the Lower Ossington Reading Series @ 135 Ossington, & Knife Fork Book @ The Great Escape Bookstore. The poem on page 71 first appeared in *Block Party*. A section from 'A Lyre' was published as a pamphlet by No Press. 'Performative Utterances' first appeared in *Echolocation*. Portions of 'A Lyre' have been published in *Doc(k)s*.

Thank you to the Canada Council for the Arts, Ontario Arts Council, & Toronto Arts Council for their financial support.

Thank you to Coach House Books for trusting in me & this book, especially Alana Wilcox, Nasser Hussain, James Lindsay, & Crystal Sikma. Thanks also to Sasha Howarth, Philip Bardach, Olivia Parker, Yanni Santos, Kate Brooks, & John De Jesus.

A special thanks, again, to Orchid Tierney for her perceptive reading & for writing the afterword to this collection.

Finally, I am never bereft of gratitude but often of words to express it. My deepest thanks to Alysha Dawn Puopolo for sharing this beautiful life.

Eric Schmaltz is the author of *Borderblur Poetics: Intermedia and Avant-gardism in Canada, 1963–1988* (University of Calgary Press) and *Surfaces* (Invisible Publishing). He is the editor of *Another Order: Selected Works of Judith Copithorne* (Talonbooks), and co-editor of *I Want to Tell You Love* by bill bissett and Milton Acorn (University of Calgary Press). His work has been published, exhibited, and performed nationally and internationally, in forums including *The Best American Experimental Writing*, BOMB, *Jacket2*, *ToCall*, and *The Capilano Review*. He lives in Kjipuktuk/Halifax, where he teaches English literature at Dalhousie University.

Typeset in Arno, Minion Variable Concept, and Dico Typewriter.

Printed at the Coach House on bpNichol Lane in Toronto, Ontario, on Zephyr Antique Laid paper, which was manufactured, acid-free, in Saint-Jérôme, Quebec, from second-growth forests. This book was printed with vegetable-based ink on a 1973 Heidelberg KORD offset litho press. Its pages were folded on a Baumfolder, gathered by hand, bound on a Sulby Auto-Minabinda, and trimmed on a Polar single-knife cutter.

Coach House Books is situated on occupied land, which is the traditional territory of several Indigenous nations, including the Mississaugas of the Credit (an Anishnabek people), the Haudenosaunee Confederacy, and the Wendat and Petun nations, and is now home to many First Nations, Inuit, and Métis people. This land is covered by the Dish With One Spoon Covenant, an agreement between different First Nations communities to share resources peacefully and equitably, and by the Two-Row Wampum, a covenant of mutual respect and non-interference between early settlers and the Haudenosaunee. The land is also subject to Treaty 13, sometimes called the Toronto Purchase, signed between the settler colonists and the Mississaugas of the Credit.

As a settler organization, we acknowledge that we have violated these treaties and agreements. We acknowledge the grievous and ongoing harm of colonialism, and we strive to work toward a future of justice and reconciliation.

Edited by Nasser Hussain
Cover design by Crystal Sikma
Interior design by Eric Schmaltz
Author photo by Sandro Pehar

Coach House Books
80 bpNichol Lane
Toronto ON M5S 3J4
Canada

mail@chbooks.com
www.chbooks.com